In Loving Memory Of

Paul Walsh of Cork, Ireland.

19.05.2008

A gift to the Charity shop
from the author himself.
All the best.

S. Walsh

CONTENTS

INTRODUCTION

Well, where do I begin?

That was the question I asked myself in 2019 when I first decided I was going to write a book.

Firstly, although I do feel it's a part of my soul, truly and authentically me, no one would've ever anticipated that I would be writing a book, not even myself.

Yet here I am, writing an introduction for the book I've written, which will absolutely be the first of many.

My purpose in writing this book is to reach people outside of my social circle, people who I never would've been able to reach without writing this. The motivation is to help others through similar struggles that I have endured, persevered through, and overcome.

Therefore, within this book, I have preached only of the actions and methods which I, myself, have practised in the past and will continue to practise to get me through any future times of turmoil.

The contents within this book have guided me through many hardships. From a home that began to break from the bad decisions of my parents, who had a Heroin addiction, to even more adversities faced growing up alone and away from family since the age of 14.

How I let my sorrows assist me in appreciating every moment. How I let my dad's death help me realise how precious life is, instead of being plagued by sadness. Of course, there's also my own actions and mistakes which have given me increased understanding.

Then rising above it all and doing well for myself for a period of time, and later on having a spell in prison.

I hope you enjoy the read ahead of you and I sincerely wish that some of my methods can be of help to you.

Mental illness health cases are rising, so it's very important that we all work on self improvement and uplift those around us, because no one is immune to being affected by mental illness.

This isn't about being perfect, this is about learning ways to be grateful for all of your imperfections and keeping yourself in a healthy conscience, regardless of your life circumstances and hardships.

Pain to Progress
Wounds to Wisdom
Troubles to Triumphs

I wanted to write this book to help those from similar backgrounds as me and for those who want to overcome mental adversity.

I advise everyone to begin reading regularly because the future is going to happen regardless. Don't you think it's wiser to face it a little smarter?

Life gets easier when your foundations get stronger. It's not rocket science, but even if it was, it would be worthwhile to partake in self improvement because it benefits your existence.

Increase and then spread your knowledge wherever you go. While some may never take notice nor reap its benefits, the knowledge you bestow upon those who listen can be massively uplifting to their spirits and you can help their lives flourish. To help even just one person out there will make all the time I invested in this book worthwhile. I hope you enjoy the read ahead of you and that some of my ways of overcoming trials and tribulations in life can assist you in overcoming problems that are personal to yourself.

Enjoy.

-Sean Atlas Walsh

Artwork by Annalise B.

1
Autopsy Your Errors

I will now explain why it is of utmost importance to practise 'autopsy your errors' during the process of elevating yourself into a better version.

Practising autopsy your errors is when you find you've made an error, then you put active effort into becoming aware of the errors origin. Now, once you locate the causes of a particular error, then you have knowledge of when and where you made the mistakes. This helps you not only limit your errors but also cancel even making them in the first place. You don't need to have everything figured out, you just need to be taking steps toward trying to improve your ways. You will do just that by recognising your errors, so you can then rectify and avoid them.

An autopsy procedure is generally associated with finding out the causes of the end of life, but with autopsy your errors, you will find it is the opposite. It's all about finding out the causes of errors and limitations, then living a better life by rectifying those errors and removing those limitations. In the process of doing so, you will live a more healthy and happy life. By acknowledging your errors of today you will better your beginnings tomorrow.

Every small action will affect your overall standard of life, your approach towards the small tasks in life will play a role in your attitude towards the more important tasks. All skyscrapers were built from the ground up, so make sure you find, then fix, all errors limiting you through autopsying your ways. It's wise to become aware of the causes of our problems because then we equip ourselves with the knowledge to avoid and prevent them.

Autopsy your life while living; this will help you with problem prevention. If my dad had done an autopsy of his errors, it's highly likely he'd still be alive. We can't and must not continue to do actions that harm or hinder us.

As I will later mention in the chapter, 'Consciousness', the more you hand pick knowledge to help aid your life, the sooner your reality will improve. By learning the initial causes of your errors, you strengthen yourself toward avoiding them and also increase your chances of progress due to having awareness of your mishaps. From this, you will begin to make the right decisions. To become aware of when you do wrong is the first step to finding the right things to do.

The autopsy of error procedure can be effectively used toward anything from small daily tasks that are incomplete, to the more important matters regarding habits that affect our health, and even locating those people who don't align with our lifestyles. The process also helps to terminate small errors that could potentially lead you to big mistakes. Small errors can lead you to limited gain and even loss of pay, while small changes in the right direction can lead up to a massive change.

I will give you an example of how you can apply autopsy your errors:

I often set out to read one chapter of a book a day but after three days of doing so, I'd miss a day. Then it would be one day reading, one day not, so an autopsy of error can be applied to even small tasks; to locate why they're incomplete or done wrong.

I applied the method of autopsy to the days I did read and I became aware of when I utilised my time and completed the reading I set out to do. More significantly, I autopsied the day I didn't read and then I found out where on those days my decisions surrounding utilising time was polluted by choosing to do other things first, which led me to be wasteful with my time.

So on the days I didn't read, I now discovered by doing a step by step autopsy of the day that the very moment I decided to go onto social media before reading, is the very moment I lose 30 minutes of task time. Of course I could've used this period more wisely, so now that I'm fully conscious of where I waste time, what do you think happens the next time I'm about to go on to social media?

I asked myself, "Sean, have you completed your daily chapter?"

Remember the more aware you are of errors, the more likely you are to stop making them. Apply autopsy of error to any scenario personal to you and you will be able to locate where mistakes are being made; resulting in you being a better and smarter version today than you were yesterday.

Another example of how autopsy of error has helped me stop doing continuous errors in oblivion is when trying to maintain consistency with physical exercise.

Instead of me going back on past experiences and trying to figure out why I didn't complete what I set out to do, and of course, why I couldn't maintain consistency, I instead just set in place an autopsy of errors on the next occasion I didn't go to the gym. I intended to stick to my plans of being consistent, and by doing so, the autopsy of my errors has helped me find all the initial causes of my downfalls on route to physical progress. By becoming aware of these errors, I prevent them from happening repetitively, and as we all commonly know, prevention is always better than a cure. My tactic is to **prevent inconsistencies,** which then **leads me to become more consistent.**

Preventing being inconsistent makes you consistent, it's simple.

You can cure, then cancel these oblivious errors the very moment you acknowledge them. After doing a daily autopsy in regard to physical progress, I then trained 451 days in a row without a single day missed. I realised that my inconsistency was due to being oblivious to my defects, and by using this method in life, SUCCESS gets a little bit easier. In this regard, as my muscles got stronger, the exercises became easier.

You will make good progress in any regard after autopsying your ways because you will become aware of your mistakes and then cancel them.

If you don't like having to rebuild from the beginning, then never stop what you're doing, remain consistent, and the momentum will make many aspects of life feel easier.

Wasting time is one of the biggest errors that the majority of us never acknowledge. We like to either choose to rest or to declare we don't have enough time to do certain things. The same people who convince themselves that they do not have enough time to read, are the same people who will spend an hour or more on social media everyday. Autopsy where you waste time, ask yourself…

If your life had a referee, would you get penalised for wasting time?

There is and always will be enough time in our daily lives to do the important things, but make sure you *correct the*

order of your priorities to enhance your own self improvement.

One massive error many people make is comparing themselves to others. I find this to be a particularly serious error. When individuals compare other people's success to their negative aspects in life, it generally does not result in them feeling good about themself. **Remember each and every person has their own unique journey through life and there is always more than meets the eye.**

Once you autopsy your ways you will begin to notice how comparing to others leads you to limit your own happiness. It leads you to become envious, it will eliminate the gratitude for the things you do have, and make you feel less than others. It could also sap you of your motivation because if you see someone else who seems to be successful with ease, all while you are struggling to make ends meet, this could end up taking away energy from your aspirations. Do **not** make the error of comparing yourself to others.

Of course it is good to have role models to look up to and want to follow in their footsteps toward success, but do not begin to compare your situation to anyone else's, as this could lead you to lose hope in your own journey. Love your own existence, push your own limits, follow your own dreams, because only YOU can become YOUR best version. Autopsy where and when you allow yourself to fall into comparison and avoid the apps that get us caught in a whirlwind of such comparisons. It's wise to keep in mind that on social media people are portraying their best version, even to the point of it sometimes all being a facade. I know this through experience, I personally know people who look like they need a helping hand but in reality are financially very successful and I know others who look like they're drowning in money on Instagram but they're struggling financially in reality. There is always more than what the eyes can see. ***Don't compare yourself to what others portray, for you could be comparing to non-reality and feeling less about yourself in the process.*** These social media apps are just highlights of people's lives; not many people add their struggles to these highlights, so do not compare your mistakes to anyone else's handpicked highlights of their life. **We all face struggles in life but don't increase yours by comparison to others.**

It's really odd when you take a step back to autopsy the ways we make ourselves feel. How can we be comparing our lesser qualities to a person's best qualities and expect to feel better or uplifted in ourselves?

Each individual has their own abilities and powers. If you compare a fish to a bird on the basis of flight, the fish will feel worthless, but if you compare the fish and the bird on their ability to swim, the bird will feel worthless.

Remember not to compare your weaknesses to other's strengths, as there is always more than meets the eye, and discover your own abilities and feel confident in yourself.

As I said, ***each and every person has their own unique journey through life, there is always more than meets the eyes.*** So focus on yourself, take the actions required to better yourself, and by doing so you will feel an increase in your self worth and confidence.

Comparing your strengths to others can also be of detriment. Why?

Because it can lead you to have an inflated ego and then you may become complacent; meaning the strengths you were comparing have become weaker. Doing an autopsy of error can lead you into so much progression, all with less effort, to find the root cause of a mishap. This enables you to cancel making the same mistakes twice.

Comparison should only be used in a positive way, such as to motivate you to follow in a successful individual's footsteps, or to hear success stories from people who have been through tough circumstances. This can allow you to compare your adversities to others similar to you, who then went on to become successful. Only compare in a positive manner and don't ever compare your inner problems with others' exterior positives. Celebrate others' successes, praise others for their triumphs and want more for yourself with daily effort toward leading the life you want to live. The more you spread positivity, the more positive you will become, and by celebrating others triumphs you will be doing just that. I see many people from the council estates I come from have genuine hate and envy for someone who has risen out of the place they have come from. This I will never understand because authentically my heart has pure intentions, and how can you not be inspired to become a better person by seeing someone elevating from the same place you came from?

Be inspired, don't become envious by comparing yourself to those who are successful, never feel less worthy when seeing others do well, and do not compare your life to anyone else's. You must first love your own life and then work towards your own development. Cheering on others will only benefit your life in many ways.

As you are improving,

and you are improving,

you'll begin to notice.

After learning what not to do, you will have more time and energy for all the more important things and you will be able to complete tasks correctly.

Progress is already on the horizon.

You can autopsy any errors you are making to locate the causes. For example, if you intend to eat more healthily but return to old habits of unhealthy eating, then you need to do a step by step autopsy of the day you made mistakes. After doing so, you will be more aware of when and why you made the wrong decisions regarding your diet. When I personally did this, I discovered that when I waited until I was hungry to choose what to eat; that was when I made the bad decisions that went against my intentions. After finding this through autopsy, I then began eating more healthily by choosing my next meal before I became hungry and this has led to me living a more positive lifestyle with a diet that is much more healthy.

I still love to treat myself more than from time to time, but the majority of the time I'm eating clean and feeling mentally stronger in the process.

Use autopsy your error when you set out to do something but don't end up doing so. This will lead you to completing more tasks and hitting targets both big and small.

Autopsy any area of your life that you feel has defects and become more aware of why you have these defects; resulting in you having more control over your own life and understanding yourself and habits better.

HABITS

You will need to do an autopsy of your habits.

Growing up in the circumstances that I did, I always associated habits as negative occurrences, but habits aren't always negative. A habit is a regular tendency of doing something and most of these tendencies are hard to give up. We can develop positive habits in life but before we attempt to increase our positive habits, it's important we acknowledge and work towards removing the negative tendencies we have developed first. Many of the habits and tendencies we have, we gained from the people we spend time with or they are simply unconscious and unaware errors.

Bad habits will interrupt your life and prevent you from achieving your goals. Locate bad habits that you have and consciously replace them with positive habits to aid you toward progression.

A very effective way of defeating a bad habit is to accept the habit and let go. Most people let the habit gain persistence by resisting to accept the habit for what it is. The moment you acknowledge the bad habit and its negative impacts, you can then accept it's no longer best for you to continue it. Then, it becomes so much easier to conquer and stop. **Don't resist change and you will change for the better.** The procedure of closely analysing your day by autopsy will assist you in noticing where and when you partake in bad habits, so you can stop wasting energy in such ways and begin developing positive tendencies.

Autopsy your error is effective at discovering the root cause of issues and finding a solution to the root cause, instead of finding solutions to an ever flowing problem. Having a solution to the problem's origin conquers the problem, and rather than letting errors and problems continue, you fix them or avoid them completely.

I want you to imagine a scenario of a person mopping and having to dry the kitchen floor each and every day because of a leaking pipe. Now, by mopping and drying the floor daily, it means it has taken daily effort to keep the kitchen dry and clean right?

But with autopsy your errors you find the root cause of an issue and correct what's causing the ever-flowing problem. So in this example, you fix the drain pipe that's leaking… then mop and dry the floor once more, to ultimately have a completely dry and clean kitchen floor.

It's about autopsying your errors, finding the root cause of the error, and then fixing the root cause instead of exerting daily energy on a continuous error that causes you defect, waste of energy, or stress.

Use this drain pipe analogy next time you're facing a daily issue. Can you fix something before the day begins to stop the problems from continuously flowing? **If so, then do so. There's nothing to lose in experimenting with how to improve**. It's worth an attempt; after all you could conquer daily troubles in the process of discovering solutions.

Don't mop the floor with daily issues if today you can fix the leak and relieve tomorrow of its troubles.

At times, all we need to do when facing difficulties is to take a step back, acknowledge that the situation is not good for us, and start fresh. This sounds like such common sense, but it isn't the most common action taken when caught up in the moment. When we are overwhelmed by problems we often struggle to notice or figure out a solution, so simply take a step back to analyse the situation, then proceed to take the action which will help alleviate both your stresses and the problem.

Upon taking a step back to acknowledge the issues and possible solutions clearly, you may even feel as if the situation that is causing you annoyance or stress isn't even worthy of your energy. For example: why hold onto resentment for someone who is no longer deserving of your emotions and attention?

A simple solution is to forgive them for yourself, forgive them to alleviate your resentment, and let go of anything that can harm your ways of thinking. Pilot yourself away from any scenarios that are undeserving of your presence.

Keeping Good Company

The truth is, many of us make the error of valuing the length of a relationship over the strength of a relationship. It doesn't mean that because we've known someone for a longer duration that they're the individuals with the best intentions for us. There is a saying that your biggest supporter is a stranger and that your biggest hater is someone you know. We need to cancel out making these errors.

We need to do an autopsy of the company we keep. In life, those who surround us play a massive role in our development as people, and many individuals who have had great potential of their own have been held back by the company they've kept over the years. This is plain to see when someone who was predicted to be prosperous was limited because their dreams were dampened by those around them.

Autopsying the company we keep isn't just about our friendship; this applies to family and even romantic partners. It is pivotal towards your progression of becoming a better person that you autopsy your company. I'm not here to advise you to become militant in life and stop communicating with those who hinder your progress, but you definitely will need to autopsy, then acknowledge, who is holding you back unintentionally and who is pushing you forward in life. After doing an autopsy, you will discover the relationships that don't align with your aspiration of improving your life. More than likely, the individuals that are holding us back don't purposely intend to do so, but in life we have to accept that sometimes we simply outgrow people. It's a sad reality but you can't remain in the same old ways if you're aspiring for change.

We will need to pay close attention to the person we engage with romantically, as we always need to be wise when choosing a partner. For one, because we will very likely be spending the majority of our time with this individual; as in our adult lives we spend the most time with our spouse and after a certain amount of time, you will eventually be living together. Secondly, you will need to ensure that you are compatible, as quite literally your partner's insecurities will soon become your problems and this could lead you to limitations. For example:

an insecure lover wouldn't ever want their partner doing modelling due to the insecurities they have within themselves. **Our romantic partner's energy will have a massive impact on us, so we need to really analyse someone's compatibility before we commit to them.** *We live in times of **more lust than love** and those who are truly loving are hard to find, but by taking your time to autopsy the compatibility and standard of a relationship, you will be giving yourself the best chance at finding someone to help you flourish in life and not diminish your progress.*

Autopsy the friends you keep.

You will need to notice where and with whom you make errors and mistakes with the most often.

You will have to change or limit time with certain friends. As I mentioned before, in life you outgrow people and even though loyalty is important, real loyal friends will also want the best for you. So if that means limiting time with each other because of conflicting pathways and/or interest, then so be it.

You can't just carry childhood friends through life if they're constantly influencing you in negative ways, you need to spend your time wisely. You have to nurture your own pathway, be a trailblazer if need be, but always be your own person. Then pay close attention to those you surround yourself with, as it is wise to have friends of similar interests to assist your progress.

List of Friends

1-

2-

3-

4-

5-

This top five friends list, which will show you who you spend most of your time with, is crucial to your environment and elevation because you will pick up on their beliefs, interests and habits.

By surrounding yourself with positive and ambitious friends who have similar interests and passions as your own, you will develop more as a person. You will share the habits of the company you keep, so choose your top 5 close companions wisely.

Birds of a feather flock together, eagles and pigeons don't fly together. Eagles are birds of prey and go hunting for their food. Pigeons, on the other hand, are happy and content with crumbs they're given and leftover food from trash cans in the city. So which would you rather be?

The eagle or the pigeon?

If we look closely, we can learn from animals and nature, although I believe in unity in humanity as a whole, in many characteristics we differ massively. There's a reason why birds of the same species stick together and why you don't see eagles flying with vultures or pigeons, because they have different means of survival and different characteristics. So, while we are all human, you need to flock with those who have the same interest and characteristics as yourself to enhance progress. Have you ever had an open-minded conversation with a close-minded person? If so, you'll understand my concept. We are all uniquely ourselves on this planet… but surround yourself with those who are like minded.

Less is More

Quality always over quantity.

Being around fewer people, but sticking with those of good and consistent ambitious character, is a million times more flourishing for a great future than living amongst a large quantity of people who never strive for more. Think of it like this: 3 eagles flying together hunting for more is better than a large group of pigeons roaming around crumb-nibbling. This isn't about changing your friendship group at all, it's more so about discovering which friends impact your progress in a positive way, and which friends hinder you from becoming your best version.

Healthy competition is always a great harvest of progress.

As we all know, having any form of competition is good for pushing oneself to do better, so having friends to compete with is a healthy way of enhancing our skills and abilities. This is exactly why successful sportsmen and women claim they wouldn't have been as skilled at their particular sport if it wasn't for the active competition they had growing up with their siblings.

I personally learned how to fight and defend myself by having fights with my older brothers, and although the bumps and bruises weren't enjoyable, nor the dog bites that I received in the middle of battle with my brothers, it's safe to say I could more than handle myself in the real world after those childhood scuffles.

All competition is good for actively making us do better, but definitely surround yourself with those of similar interest of your own, as this will ensure you further develop.

There is a difference between healthy competition and toxic or negative competition. Toxic competition can sometimes cause more harm than help because it is fuelled by jealousy or hate. Instead of building each other up and developing, the situation can turn sour and you can end up being dragged down by those you are competing with. Especially with them saying negative things and criticising you, remember those that compete with toxic tendencies will say whatever they can to get an advantage. So don't partake or take notice of those people and stay healthy.

After practising autopsy your errors, you will soon realise it's much better to do one thing at a time perfectly, than to do multiple things improperly. The bird that hatched from an egg in a nest high up in the tree needs to focus initially on how to fly, or else the chick will fall from the nest to a premature death. So in life, do not make errors by focusing on more than what you need to. Rather, do less but to a higher standard, because quite literally one small step in a positive direction daily will impact your life massively.

Don't make errors by trying to do more than what's required, focus on what is in your control, then do all things to a higher standard. Less is more, 3 good friends is better than 10 bad ones. 3 jobs well done will boost your reputation more than 10 jobs done poorly in haste.

Less is more.

The **purpose of this chapter** is to help us find our defects, improve our ways of living, and better our futures through **problem prevention**. Upon putting this chapter to practise, you will stop making small errors that can lead to big mistakes. Even if we are striving and doing well, there are always more ways through which we can improve ourselves.

"Every person of a prestigious position has had a past, and every person who is living in an earthly hell has a future, but only by locating and correcting their errors and revolutionising their ways, will they find themselves evolving into a better version. As we know, the future is going to happen regardless, so let's find and then fix our errors through autopsy, improve daily and to the best of our abilities be prepared for future opportunities."
-Sean Walsh

Artwork by Romario L.

2

MENTAL PILOT

Take back control, don't be on autopilot when some of the things you do
continuously harm you.

First and foremost, I want you to establish that you are your own mental pilot...

This isn't to say you're fully responsible for every situation you've been in. For sometimes in life, just like with storms, troubles arise with no warning or cause of our own but it is to state that you are responsible for steering yourself away from turbulence, and ultimately it is you who decides how to react to things.

"Our reactions are more important than what has actually happened, for what's happened is in the past and our reactions now determine our futures."

- Sean Atlas Walsh

Instead of dwelling on the negative happenings, instead focus all your attention on your reactions, because this will not only help you to avoid pondering on the painful problems of the past, but it will also ensure you don't let the turmoil you have faced thieve you of a much brighter future. How do you think people gain good outcomes from negative circumstances?

They do so with positive reactions and you could also do so with mental guidance,

By accepting self accountability for how you feel mentally, you will instantly begin to guide yourself to do more things in life that result in positivity. Do not blame past happenings for your present suffering; with good reactions we can overcome even the worst situations.

You are liable for the actions you take, which result in how you have felt in the past and how you feel in current and future situations.

If you were flying a plane you wouldn't head towards turbulent areas on purpose, so don't do actions in life that cause you mental adversity either. It sounds like such common sense but for those people facing adversities off the back of their actions, they fail to see the causes of their ongoing mental turbulence.

I will give you an example of this:

I had friends who had never experienced paranoia in their lives up until they began smoking marijuana. Now, if they were aware of being their own mental pilot back then, as soon as they tried marijuana (which was something new to them) these people would've acknowledged that for them smoking cannabis was increasing their paranoia and heightening their anxieties. Unfortunately they blindly continued to partake in exactly what is causing their suffering. By becoming your own mental pilot and analysing the effects of your actions, you will leap towards a life of less hardships alongside giving yourself the best chance of success.

YOU are **YOUR** own personal pilot because, in all honesty, what works for one person can damage another. So you need to personally analyse what works for you. Have you ever asked yourself how or why the exact same joint and strain of marijuana will calm one person's nerves and heighten both their positive and creative ways; while for another person it shakes their mental stability, heightens their anxieties and has them overthinking negatively?

This is because we all experience things uniquely. We all have to be our own mental pilots because ***no one can give us better advice than we can analyse and advise ourselves!***

People who don't analyse or guide themselves mentally can get very useful advice from external sources such as counsellors or friends and family, but it's important we begin to acknowledge how we feel after trying different things in life. This will help us discover what works well with us, and what once had a bad effect both mentally and physically on us. This will lead us toward a life of less adversity and more energy to do what we feel best doing.

We individually need to pilot ourselves mentally and be aware of what increases our difficulties and also of what works very well for us personally.

Keep in mind what works for you might not work for those in your friend group, but always be true to yourself. **There is no sacrifice more worthy and important than that which aids your health.**

Only you have the power to steer yourself daily in the right direction, **find healthy coping mechanisms for times of tribulations and run a trial of how you feel after experiencing new things.** Become aware of what has a good impact on you and what's of detriment.

As you you getting to know yourself better
And you are getting to know yourself,
You will begin to notice.

It is important to try new activities and hobbies to conquer boredom because when we become bored we often end up doing something that isn't good for us or we can begin to overthink situations from the past. If you're lacking inspiration of what new things you can try, well even Facebook has an interest section that is full with hundreds of hobby options which can later become passions.

It's all about finding what's for you personally and then utilising these new found hobbies and passions to pilot you smoothly through life's ups and downs. You will experience less boredom after discovering new interests, which will mean you'll avoid falling into negative ways by doing something positive that you enjoy, rather than being bored and overthinking.

You will find comfort in turbulence with being your own mental pilot because you will have the awareness of what actions have a good impact on you. So, you can consciously choose what to do to assist you through difficulty.

Mental pilot also consists of ensuring that you are well prepared for the day.

You can plan and prepare your day before it begins. This will cancel or limit the stresses of certain things, and while this isn't about anticipating stress or manifesting negative scenarios, it is about preparation surrounding the future aspects of the day that will take place. For example, you wouldn't leave picking out the outfit for a special day until an hour before you need to be at the venue...right? Contemplate how much stress that would cause you. Instead, most people will prepare and plan what to wear ahead of schedule to save themselves that last minute pressure and mental adversity.

This is how we should guide ourselves mentally; we shouldn't allow situations to increase our mental diffculties due to lack of preparation. So quite literally with **preparation comes peace.** When I look after my sister's sons (my best friends!), who are young, I make the babysitting easier by preparing my house for the sleepover with pre-made milk bottles. As soon as Zayden, who is 1, wakes for his late night feed it's 30 seconds in the microwave and then there's no stress. He's happy and we're back to sleep. **All aspects that will definitely take place in the future we have no excuse to not plan or prepare for.** It will cancel or alleviate the stress of future pressure.

We have to ensure we keep ourselves in the best possible position to feel strong, energetic and happy. We will do just that by consciously becoming our own mental pilots.

I have a question for you...

Do you expect to feel perfect while living out most of your days dehydrated?

Would you expect your car to function properly without engine oil? Or even worse yet, expect your car to drive with no fuel?

It is unrealistic to expect your car to get you to your destination with no fuel.

As it is unrealistic to expect to feel at your best while not maintaining hydration.

Do not expect to feel mentally energetic, physically strong and happy when not maintaining the hydration our bodies require to function properly.

Next time you have a headache, find yourself feeling down emotionally or feel physically fatigued, don't look for external things to blame, do a **human engine check** and give yourself the best chance by keeping fuelled for the day ahead. You'll be surprised at the difference of simply maintaining proper hydration. Aim for 2-3 litres of Spring Water per day minimum.

I always express to people that maintaining ourselves physically and mentally is a form of progression in itself. If you ask a person who has sadly declined mentally if he wishes that he could have maintained a level headed way of thinking, what do you think his answer would be?

Or the same if you asked an individual who began to fall short in her efforts of physical exercise due to inconsistencies; if she could have simply maintained the consistency would she be in a better physical position currently?

Allow the answers of these 2 questions to show you that maintenance is an act of progression.

Mental maintenance is a form of progression. Don't lose your balance by constantly seeking more than what you're comfortable with or by not appreciating your current circumstances.

Do not fall victim to self-diagnosis, as many individuals increase their mental difficulties by convincing themselves that they're less than others, or that they have too many problems to overcome, or even that they are not able to do something. Do not self-diagnose anything negative upon yourself. We are all able to improve on our ways, but **the moment you declare that you're tired, you instantly feel more tired**. It's natural for energy to fluctuate but don't increase the fatigue by always saying that you're tired, as this could even affect others around you. It will most definitely make you feel more tired as soon as you declare so, and many of the smaller tasks become much more difficult when you decide you haven't got the energy. In reality you do physically have the energy but mentally you've self-diagnosed tiredness long before you became physically fatigued. This is why as my own mental pilot I know for a fact through experience that at times we mentally try to convince ourselves we haven't got the energy, but when I pushed past the self-diagnosing thoughts of tiredness I proceeded to go to the gym and workout extremely hard. Let this example of the thoughts of tiredness express to you that they're just the thoughts that want to keep you in comfort, but they're aren't really that comfortable after all because preserving physical and mental energy will have you awake late at night and affect your patterns of sleep. Do not allow thoughts to limit you or make you feel as if you haven't got the energy to do what you really want to.

Be your own enthusiastic mental pilot.

Another action I have found that uplifts me mentally is the action of helping others. I have never done good for others with the hopes to make myself feel better, but as a reward for the genuine help I have provided to people in the past, I have always felt mentally and spiritually uplifted after doing so. Treat people accordingly, but help as many people as possible, because you never know what someone is truly going through. I think it is better to live life by being kind to all until you have a reason not to, instead of choosing to not be kind and helpful to others unless they deserve it. What I mean by this is, we are taught to avoid strangers and not to speak with people we don't know, yet wasn't your best friend once a stranger?

Even your romantic partner was once a stranger.

One conversation can conquer a lonely person's loneliness, so uplift others at every chance you get. Life is difficult at times and we can never guess what someone else is going through.

Be kind to all, kindness is never a weakness, and I consider kindness a strength!

By being kind to others you will spiritually and mentally feel uplifted in the process, and when doing good actions, it will result in more mental strength and happiness.

Compatibility

You will always need to analyse beyond beauty. **Do not give into the lust you feel at the cost of your mental stability**, just because the person is pretty and pleasing to the eye, that shouldn't push you to commit towards a situation that is incompatible with you.

You will never buy a car by viewing just the exterior. You'll want to get a full engine check and find out what's beneath the bonnet before you commit to the purchase. Do the same with people before you commit to any form of relationship. It's important that you do this as it will guide you away from potential mental disturbances and will prevent you from committing to bad relationships.

You can become a prisoner even if you were never sentenced by a judge. Stop committing to love with an individual who doesn't want the best for you, as they will begin to imprison your visions and limit you. Always analyse beyond the beauty and make sure there is compatibility.

I have seen many of my associates in the past who were mentally stable and ambitious fall into love because of lust and then end up in adverse circumstances; all because they committed themselves towards something that wasn't right for them. Do not commit to situations without analysing and testing the compatibility.

Be your own mental guide and you will feel so much better in your daily life.

Balance is a very important part of development and as your own mental pilot you will need to find balance to stabilise your journey through life.

One thing that's better than balance is harmony, but getting things into balance is the first step to finding harmony because when you are balanced you will learn which parts of life you can increase, decrease or combine to complement one another.

I say harmony is better than balance because you may personally require more of one aspect of life than the other, so in that regard perfect balance wouldn't be ideal. Aim for balance first and then you will be able to analyse your life. Then do less or more of whatever you feel is uniquely harmonious for you.

You become more harmonious when simply doing what makes you happier and being consistent with your days. It's important to have plans with the intention to execute them, as this will give you increased mental focus with your intentions for the day ahead.

You will heighten progression with a life of balance and harmony, for you will know what needs to be done in the present moment and you will have enough time daily to complete what you planned, prepared and intended.

Harmony amongst others is crucial for well-being, as it will cancel or limit conflicts which would have definitely drained your energy. It's simple, if one person in your life is ruining the harmony that you seek, they need to be removed.

No denying it, at times it is painful to cut ties, but there are not many sacrifices more worthy than the sacrifices made to improve your harmony.

The process of acquiring true harmony in life isn't always easy, so don't expect everything to fall into place with ease. **However, for the purpose of gaining happiness it is worth going through difficulties**, and we need to acknowledge that it is through our struggles that we get to know ourselves more deeply. Target a life of harmony as soon as possible because it will ensure stability in your life. To put a puzzle together it takes trying different pieces in different places, so don't be shy to add or remove aspects of your life throughout the learning process.

Think of this, for new furniture to fit through doorways it may need to be broken down and rebuilt again, so never avoid having to remove or add aspects of your life at times. People from the past will assume that they know you but after becoming the pilot of your mentality and rebuilding yourself into a newfound positive person, you will even keep yourself guessing because many unexpected forms of progression will be on the horizon.

Some people continue to live their lives in unstable and emotionally painful ways; all because they fail to realise that they need to mentally focus on how and why they're feeling the way that they do. After analysing your thoughts, feelings and emotions you will have a deeper understanding of yourself. Autopsy your foundations and ways of living, and with more self understanding you will be well on course to rebuilding yourself as an improved and more stable person. **Always pay attention to your mental health and be your own guidance.**

Suppress Anger

Now, suppressing anger is a crucial part of being your own pilot. Avoid getting into situations where your emotions can get the better of you.

Self control will be needed, as anger can be one of the hardest emotions to contain, and if you consider yourself a person who gets angry easily I'd highly suggest for you to do a course regarding anger management. It will save you a lot of trouble and time. As I write this in manuscript form, I am currently in prison for letting anger take control of me in a situation where I felt I needed to defend myself, yet if I controlled my anger in that very encounter I would have my freedom right now.

So if I was able to suppress the anger I felt, I would be still living in the free world.

Do not allow anger to result in a loss for you and others. In my situation we both lost because I lost my freedom and all 3 of the other people got injured.

Now although I do feel like I was simply defending myself, I could've easily and more wisely attempted to walk away. Yet, as I said, anger is one of the hardest emotions to feel and contain, especially when fighting feels like second nature, and yet I still must accept that I made the wrong decisions in that moment.

Admitting to accepting that you can't control your anger is admitting to the fact you can't control yourself. Still, acceptance is the first step to self improvement because many people don't even acknowledge where and how they have done or gone wrong.

Whether the anger stems from past experiences, pride, spirit, or from our egos, we need to suppress it in order to truly gain control of ourselves.

Anger is a punishment you allow yourself to feel for the actions of someone else. Don't allow people to make a puppet out of you and more importantly, don't let others tempt you into doing things that are detrimental to your improvement.

So if you feel an anger management course will benefit you in any way then most definitely do it; don't learn the hard way.

If I was advised to do so before losing my freedom, then I would've been able to tame my temper, and all of these emotions are natural to us as humans, so we must learn how to manage and control them to become better people.

"The strongest person can't be determined by how much weight they can lift in the gym. Real strength can be measured by how much a person is in control of their actions, feelings and emotions. With Mental Pilot, you become more aware of how to be in control of yourself, and then you can pilot yourself into progression and ultimately avoid transgressions."-Sean Walsh

"The tongue needs orchestration because the tongue can strike once and sting the mind forever." -Sean Walsh

I was taught by my dad from a young age, may he rest in perfect peace, that we should be kind to people because we don't know the struggles or situations that people are going through. As I expressed with my quote above, one word can infect someone's mind for many years. A punch we can heal from quickly, but hurtful words can sink into our minds and harm us continuously.

We must learn to hold back our tongues when angry because you can't take back words and their impacts once spoken, and the tongue can harm a person more mentally than a fist can harm physically. The tongue can leave scars on the soul with its sharpness and harm someone's spirit; words can have long lasting impacts and could take a lot of effort to heal from, more than it will take to heal from physical inflictions.

Do not talk to your parents rudely; they taught you how to speak.

It doesn't matter how angry or annoyed you are, under no circumstances shall you be rude to your elderly loved ones, as they taught you how to communicate in the first place. When I was younger, growing up in primary school and secondary school, it was of maximum annoyance to see other pupils talking rudely to their parents.

Firstly, because by the age of 9, my dad had already died and after hugging his head in the coffin box, I from that very moment wished I could've had one more second of time with him.

Secondly, because I have a mum who has such a good heart but couldn't do everything she wanted as a parent due to problems with heroin addiction. Never be rude to your parents, regardless of anything they do. They raised you and on top of all of that I used to see kids with what would be regarded as parents that are perfect and still they spoke at times with rudeness.

Stopping yourself from speaking while angry will alleviate the situation of its tension, prevent further internal harm of others and prevent escalation in an argument. By simply holding back your tongue you will be avoiding a more hostile scenario.

Commonly known, prevention is always better than a cure. Pilot yourself away from turbulent places where a problem may arise, as to avoid even feeling anger is better than having to feel and then suppress anger. I know this first hand through many of my previous fighting encounters.

An individual that is angry can make a statement that they don't even truly mean, but those words within that statement will still settle on the soul of the other person. This is why it is important we orchestrate our tongues and avoid saying things in moments of anger.

I will give you an example of how speaking in anger can harm those around you.

We will all experience anger at different situations in life and it can be like feeling a fire within us; but why burn others with the flame that we ourselves don't enjoy feeling?

The example I will express is this: imagine there is a father who has had a long day at work, yes indeed he hasn't had the best of days. Just one of those days when everything seems to go wrong, but now he has come home, and he could've left his anger at the doorstep and not polluted his homely environment with the annoyances from the workplace, but he didn't suppress his anger and now his son is playing football in the sitting room just kicking the ball around softly. The dad has a bad headache after the day he has experienced, and he asks his son to stop once but, as with children on many occasions, they don't listen the first time and the boy continues playing and now the father's

workplace anger has hit its limit. Even at home he can't
seem to find any comfort, so he raises his voice and shouts
to his son,
"You will never be a footballer so stop playing football right
now, stop having dreams that you're going to be a footballer
because it's not likely to ever happen."
Now, do you see how speaking in anger can kill the dreams
of those around us, because even though the dad doesn't
truly mean what he said in anger, his tongue has still sliced
and shattered the dream of his child. The son now starts to
believe internally that he is reaching too high when aspiring
to become a footballer.
One statement from a father in anger has impacted the
child's faith in himself for the future.
The tongue needs to be orchestrated always, but even more
so when feeling anger within us.
**So many relationships with genuine potential for happy
futures,have been left in ruins by the tongue being used
as a sword in arguments**. One statement in anger can
literally remain as a burden on someone for many years, and
this is why I say the tongue and the use of our words is much
more dangerous than weapons.
I truly believe that the tongue can cause more wounds than a
fist; this is why mind games are highly important in the fight
industry and all sports.
We really do need to gauge what we're going to say before
we say things, as we could obliviously be harming our
companions by speaking without thinking.
Do not speak in anger, rather orchestrate the tongue to
silence, it's better than saying statements you do not mean.
Very often after the anger has passed you will be apologetic
and ask for forgiveness, but by suppressing the tongue while
angry, you'll cause less harm to others and also avoid

escalating a problem. Then you won't have to convince the individual that you didn't mean what you mentioned.

Words are so powerful.

A truthful statement can cancel belief in a lie.

A statement of explanation can instantly end a long lasting misunderstanding.

A genuine apology written wholeheartedly can assist the victim toward forgiving the one who harmed them.

A few nicely chosen words of encouragement can leave a person with increased faith in themselves for many years to come.

Be careful with the way you use your tongue and the words you choose to speak, for the way you communicate does impact people's feelings. Do not speak in anger because you won't choose the right things to say and end up regretting the statements you made.

"Holding back your words while in anger will save you many moments of regret and sorrow for the harm you have inflicted on others."

As I previously mentioned, words can not be taken back once spoken, as the bullets can't be reversed once shot. It's the same way that harmful words can't be forgotten because the harm is done as soon as the words leave your mouth. Words can be used so positively to uplift your loved ones and even to boost a stranger's emotions, so do not blindly fire words when speaking.

You could either use your tongue as a magic wand bestowing blessings upon others or you could use your tongue like an invisible weapon which badly affects people. **The tongue's impact can have an individual feeling like a victim of their own thinking, when in reality they're a victim of the sour words someone has said to them.**

A real sign of mental progression is being able to control oneself in ways you never could before. I hope this chapter can help you become more aware of what's for you and what isn't.

Always pay close attention to your mental state and keep your mind in a healthy place.

Having self control makes you the captain of your future; do more of what is aligned with you and don't take part in anything that is of detriment to you or others.

You will heighten your self-respect by being your own mental pilot, you will not doubt yourself anymore, and your overall well-being will improve massively.

If I could better myself by being my own mental pilot then so can you.

JENGA

Do not hold a facade of strength when really you feel like you're breaking. Sometimes in life, just like with the board game JENGA, with each piece removed that keeps us stable, we get one step closer to breaking completely. Yet we also grow a step closer to being rebuilt stronger, back to our best full version. Do not feel sorry for yourself if you feel like you're breaking down, as you may need a section of pain and sorrow to squeeze the best out of you and to then push you toward bettering your ways. I recently heard a discussion on a podcast about an idea called 'THE REGION-BETA PARADOX' and to sum it up briefly, it's an idea based on studies that sometimes worse situations can be better than good situations. I'll give you an example to back up the bizarre statement I have just written.

Let's say you're with a romantic partner and when times are good, they're really good but when times get bad you can't imagine anything worse. So, because of the percentage of good times, you remain with the partner for 10 years, but within that 10 years, on average you've had one week good and one week bad. So if the initial situation was worse to begin with and there was less positive surrounding the negative, the worse situation could've actually been better for you as an individual. That's because you wouldn't have remained around a partner who was inconsistent and didn't make you entirely happy, so instead of remaining around a 50/50 situation, it would've been better for you if you were faced with more adverse circumstances to begin with. Another example could be that someone who has always experienced great comfort throughout their childhood and has never been without their parents now ends up living alone and is completely lost without their comfort or guidance. You see, **in life I know firsthand from my own experiences that some of the worst-case scenarios can install a strength in us that we wouldn't have had without the tough experiences**.

So remember, sometimes a situation that is slightly worse to begin with can be better for your life in the long run. Do not be afraid to break down and rebuild yourself.

By going through and feeling mental turmoil, when times return to normal you will be able to notice that your daily life isn't that bad after all. On many occasions I couldn't quite put my finger on the reasons for the ways I was feeling, and then a scenario of something really worth stressing arose and I ended up wishing I could go back to how I was before the scenario happened. So mentally acknowledge there is always a more adverse circumstance to be in and we shouldn't have to go through worse to appreciate where we now stand.

We can instantly strengthen ourselves by simply realising that struggles will increase our resilience, and it will also assist us in appreciating when things go well because after enduring the difficulties we will empirically know the difference.

Being your own mental pilot will result in true balance and harmony, and with increased levels of balance, you will increase your mental stability. There will be no space for uncertainty, but even more importantly, when you have a stable lifestyle you can easily observe new things you try and then run a trial of the impacts with clearer observation and understanding.

Guiding yourself mentally and being observant on how things affect you will have you in much more control over your lifestyle and you will be able to notice when and where times get turbulent. Then simply do your best to avoid the things causing you mental adversity or know the aspects of life you may need to do away with in order to alleviate your burdens. You will further your self awareness because you will know what needs to be removed due to its negative impacts, but you will also become aware of what works well and can be used to guide you through future turmoil.

You will find happiness, progress and fulfilment in creating a lifestyle of harmony.

When living a life of balance and harmony you will improve your overall standard of life. You will have the time required to look out for yourself completely, and finally, after years of convincing yourself you didn't have the time to cook and eat healthily, look into business proposals, exercise or even some time for meditation; with a life of balance and harmony you will have time to do all of these very important things all while ensuring you are physically, mentally, spiritually and economically stable.

As I mentioned, finding true balance is a learning process, so mentally pilot yourself through new ways of living and analyse yourself to understand how you're affected or feeling by certain aspects of the life you live.

You are in charge of your own existence. Never feel like you're limited to one way of living because it is our duty to try new ways of living, then locate the ways in which we feel happiest or the place we feel we are destined to be.

I want you to acknowledge the fact of how the prices are different in different places, and it is the exact same way we can feel happier, more valued and loved in different places. You see, in petrol stations items are more expensive right? Or when you're buying food at the airport everything has increased in price.

So what I'm getting at here is, if you feel unloved, unwanted, unhappy and as if no matter what methods you apply to your life nothing changes, it could be that you are in an environment where you will never find mental satisfaction, so you may need to fly yourself somewhere else to find the mental happiness you have longed for.

I will explain further what I mean by this.

Now, let's imagine you are living in a hot country where the sun shines all year round. Will a sun bed shop exist in such a place?

No, but if it did it wouldn't do well at all because the shop will be in a location where it's purpose is pointless, because the sun shines daily in that location. Yet if you take that same sun-bed shop idea to the countries that lack sun all through the winter months, it will likely be overwhelmed with customers.

Same shop, different place, with massively improved importance and purpose.

The same way a location impacts the purpose of a business idea, is the same way a location can impact our feeling of self worth and purpose. I know we all don't have the means to up and leave the country we live in with ease, but if you're continually unhappy and nothing seems to brighten up your feelings, a change of location could be just what you're needing.

You don't even have to change the country completely. I've often made small adjustments which had a big influence on the ways I was feeling mentally. You can change gym locations and see if you have a refreshed mental feeling. Individuals who have felt their spirit at unease, born in small cities across the globe, find their true purpose in exploring and travelling the world. With mental pilot you analyse new ways of living and observe how these changes have impacted your emotions, thoughts and feelings.

Find out what aligns best within you and do more of what feels right to you. It goes back to the simple but powerful saying of **"just do what makes you happy."**

If you feel undervalued it could be because you are giving too much of yourself to the circumstances you're in. I'm not advising you to up and leave the situation you're in, but what I do want to get across to you as my reader is that **everything in life requires balance**.

Relationships require balance to thrive. Too much time with even a loved one can become daunting, but with a little absence injected into a relationship, the heart can become more fond of the person it has missed. When you give your all to someone they can begin to not appreciate the gift of your presence, but it goes deeper than a partner's change of appreciation. During the covid lockdown period many marriages which were once flourishing, happy and harmonious, lost their thriving balance of work-life, home-life and entertainment.

Then, in the process, the marriage hit times of hardship. This happened to many people, even family homes became more difficult because too much time together and a shuffle in the routines of those living with one another, led to arguments and fallouts between siblings.

Let this show you that harmony is important but also that you may need to create a more balanced relationship in order to make sure both yourself and your partner feel truly valued.

Many individuals only acknowledge what they have had once it has been lost, so instead of noticing the value of what you have once lost, inject some absence into your relationship to help both yourself and your partner understand how much you really mean to each other.

The difference in price on items in different places is due to how much the item is in circulation...

So, to increase your value, don't be too easy to have around, even when things are so good and you completely love one another, it's still significant to maintain the balance because **everything flourishes more when kept in balance.**

Too much of even a good thing can become bad. Fruits are sweet, healthy and nutritious but too much fruit and it becomes unhealthy and upsets our stomachs.

Even bad things done in balance can lose their negative impacts. For example, alcohol is a drink considered unhealthy, which can also increase problematic situations when people make drunken errors, but even with something unhealthy, if it's done in a balanced way, it can lose all of the negative impacts. Occasional drinking could increase your enjoyment and have you enjoying the environment with a slightly altered perception and installation of confidence, and the same applies to when you're eating healthy. One cheat meal out of 10 days of eating healthy will not impact you badly, and it could actually mentally assist you toward resisting food temptations on the days you are eating healthy, because you are aware you have a cheat day that is soon approaching. This can mentally make dieting just a little bit easier.

Always remember that you are your own unique mental guide. Don't be hard on yourself if you sometimes make mistakes. Good things in excess can become bad and bad things occasionally can lose their negative impacts.

Create a balance of life that feels authentic to you, then see what else you're able to do that doesn't sacrifice the stability you have created.

At times we need to be kindly selfish to maintain the balance we have created for ourselves. All things require balance to allow stability and perfect harmony, and if we allow our balance to be impacted by others then we lose out on being our best version.

Once we have mental stability we can analyse the causes of turbulence with more understanding and clarity.

You will need to be aware of places and scenarios in which you become more worrisome. When piloting yourself to improvement you will need to acknowledge which places bring unnecessary mental turbulence and then proceed to avoid such places or to not put yourself in scenarios that cause you mental annoyance.

As you are making progress,

And you are making progress,

You'll begin to notice.

Goals and Targets

We are often advised on how setting goals and targets can be pivotal in assisting us to attain what we want to achieve, but what actually makes goals and targets so important? There are so many advantages and benefits to setting goals and having targets to hit.

Firstly, goals will keep you mentally focused and heighten your self-improvement due to having your eyes set on your aspirational achievements. This is complete mental focus on the road to success and self development.

The goals you set don't need to be humble or boring. Make them exciting; with ambitious goals and targets you can catapult yourself toward success, and even if you fall short of what you aimed for, you will find yourself in a better position.

You will further your self-understanding when achieving something that is challenging. Many people live out the same routines week after week, from paycheck to paycheck, without ever even striving for more than what they're already receiving. By setting goals and targets you will ensure that you'll be pushing to gain more from life than you are already obtaining.

As our own mental pilots, we will need to guide ourselves away from pointless distractions and maintain our mental focus. We can do exactly that by setting goals and targets. This will stop our mental energy from being wasted in the wrong places.

Mentally having a plan to work towards can limit the difficulty of hardships or will assist us in perseverance. It's all positive to set goals and targets because they will also keep us grounded and humble when things do begin to flourish. Target setting will help increase your mental energy on the road to attaining your goals, so it is relevant that you set both goals and targets to elevate your mindset. This will increase your resilience in times of hardship and will even keep you working hard when things begin to fall into place, because you will become aware that there is still more to achieve. The truth is with lofty goals and targets, you will become increasingly persistent with your approach and effort towards attaining them. **You will become more persistent in striving for success, which could never be a bad thing**. You will become an individual who will be renowned for the effort, the resilience, and the persistence you have on the road to achieving your ambitions.

You will also pay no mind to thoughts of doubt or discouragement because you will be entirely focussed on the action required for achievement.

Setting goals is a very powerful way of increasing your motivation, and with improved motivation, your performance in whatever profession you are doing will grow alongside your willingness to work and stay improving.

If you set your goals and targets high enough you will never become complacent, for you will be aware that there is always more to accomplish!

You will instantly gain more mental clarity with this understanding. Then, you can set goals and targets toward your ambitions.

Targets are very important; armies wear different colours in battle to ensure their snipers don't target their own people. What will have a higher success rate: someone shooting targets while guessing? Or a sniper who has studied and then set targets on the opposition?

In life, we likely won't be aiming rifles at enemies but we can learn from such analogies of how crucial it is that we set targets and understand what we are aiming for. This will increase our chances of success and provide us with a sense of direction.

Clarity is critical in removing any confusion you have regarding your pathway to obtaining your desires.

You will have increased mental commitment because you are now aware of what it is you are aspiring to achieve, and even when times get tough you will see the bigger picture. That means persevering through the difficulty gets a little bit easier and this will assist you on your route to completing goals and reaching targets. No time wasted in confusion and no time for doubt to dampen your commitment.

A method I have used to enhance my own and my loved ones' progression is to set challenging targets for each other instead of always setting our own comfortable goals. Sometimes we set a target that doesn't put us under pressure to achieve; it's as if we are looking out for ourselves, and this is why I say it's a good tactic to allow loved ones to set some targets for you and vice versa. For example, with weightlifting although I train as hard as I always can (and I do set good targets for my personal training performance) I sometimes can set targets short of my full capabilities. I'm normally the one leading the training sessions for my friends, so it's rare that I receive targets or challenges from others. But oh wow, I learned the hard way that I could've been doing more and pushing myself further. I learned this by training with someone much more physically developed than myself. Without ease I kept up with the workout but this showed me I am capable of loftier targets than I set for myself because with that training session, through the difficulty, I still got the work done and worked much harder than if I had set that session's targets for myself. These challenging targets will assist you in working harder than ever before, and upon completing these challenges you will be building your resilient mindset against difficulty, while piloting yourself into a better position to be successful.

DEADLINES!

Deadlines are an aspect of work or study that not many people enjoy. Most who are working and studying do not like deadlines as it puts extra pressure on them. I want to express how having deadlines set in place can quite literally be the biggest, most influential cause of your success...
Ask yourself, if those deadlines weren't put in place, would you have completed what you did within the same time span?
Most likely not, in fact you could still get the work done but it may use another month of your time that it didn't need to. That's time you could've used on something else you've been wishing you had the time to do. So, setting deadline dates for completion could massively improve your mental effort towards completing what needs to be done.

The pressure of deadlines could be exactly what you need to take action. Keep this in mind next time you feel mental pressure from something…

The pressure that is bothering you is the exact same pressure that will squeeze the best performance out of you.

Setting goals and targets with deadline dates can help you with time management. You will be able to notice if you've been wasting time or you will utilise the little spaces of time you once let go to waste. Remember as your own mental pilot you will be guiding yourself away from difficulties and with utilising your time better you will be avoiding becoming overwhelmed by pressure.

You can set deadlines for each small task and complete them one by one; this will have you step by step ascending toward your best version.

Deadlines shouldn't make you begin to work in hasty ways, but by setting dates for completion you will begin to utilise your time wisely. For example, even with this very book you're reading, this is my first time writing and I never wanted to set a deadline date because this is my first experience self-publishing. However, at this moment, I have set a deadline for the publishing date of this book to help mentally guide me to push for the book's completion. I have **purposefully made myself a prisoner of progression.** What I mean by this is, I lock myself away from distractions to ensure I complete what I have set out to accomplish, and in the shortest space of time possible.

It is ironic that as I currently write this section I'm sitting in a cafe in a nice location, but my car has limited time in the parking spot, so I am quite literally pressured to be productive during these 90 minutes. It is because of the time limit I am making the most of every moment I have in this cafe. This further expresses how deadlines and limits can pressure you to make pure progress with no time wasted. Make the most of every moment you have. We should do this in a progressive way, but also in times of enjoyment you should cherish and utilise every moment.

After you have set your aspirations in place, you will improve your mental stability instantly, as you will have a newfound sense of direction and purpose.

PURPOSE

Purpose is pivotal in regard to mental stability, and this is exactly how religions provide millions with peace!

As your own mental pilot you will need to begin at once to locate your purpose because this will provide your life with direction. As with each plane that is set to take flight, direction is needed to make sure they end up landing where intended.

Each individual's purpose can be as unique as their fingerprints, so be truthful about the life you want to lead and then steer yourself towards who you wish to become or where you wish to be.

It is significant to your mentality to be aware of your purpose. Why?

One, because you will feel like your life has meaning and you exist for a reason.

Two, simply ask someone who lacks purpose how they're feeling...

They are more often than not lost and depressed because these individuals have the mentality of 'what is the point of all of this anyway.' So, by having a purpose, you conquer the potential of being pessimistic and all while increasing your mental positivity.

Do not convince yourself that there will be a better time to begin and stop waiting for perfection and put active effort in the direction of living the life you want to lead.

So many people persuade themselves that they are simply waiting on better timing. I believe each day is a chance at making progression.

Success in my opinion is an active effort towards something you desire, attempting achievements, or doing something you've always wanted to do,

A mother who has always wanted children is a success in life due to living out her purpose.

The rich business man who dreamed of financial freedom is a success.

The football coach who doesn't get paid the most but loves and takes pride in training practice for the players is a success; for he's earning a living while following his purpose and passion.

Success comes from within. It is something truly personal to each and every person, and although we have society-based views on what is a success and what's a failure, ultimately it comes down to how one feels within. Remember, if you do what you love for work you'll never spend a day working, and doing what you love for work will cancel your dread of the day ahead. Follow your inner drives; you are your own king or queen and you decide your direction of flight.

You are the pilot of your life.

Hard work is hard, so don't always expect instant rewards, as this could stop you from enjoying what you're doing. Don't become mentally attached to the rewards you may receive at the end. Develop a growth mindset and learn to get a sense of pleasure from the hard work and effort itself, rather than always keeping your head set on the final rewards and results. Upon developing a growth mindset, you will get a daily dosage of dopamine by doing any form of progression. With a growth mindset you will also feel pure motivation when seeing others do well, because you know with your own hard work you can achieve anything you set your intentions to. Instead of feeling envy of others mentally, when you see something luxurious you will feel highly motivated. **At some of the hardest mental stages of my life I used serotonin and dopamine fasting to uplift me out of near depression. I used going to the gym daily to increase the release of the much needed dopamine, but for me serotonin is quite literally the antidote to depression.** Serotonin is crucial in my life in regards to stabilising the way I feel. When I go 3 days with no serotonin it's likely the longest, most mentally adverse 3 days I could experience. I think as we all try to better develop ourselves into a better version, we should all study (even if only briefly) the importance and role of neurotransmitters within our nervous system and the way these chemicals are responsible for the maintenance of our well-being and bodily functions.

The gym and football helped me release a lot of pent-up anger from deep within. By being my own mental pilot, I was able to analyse this and then continue to do the things that resulted in me feeling uplifted. **Now you have the purpose of being your own mental pilot, which will assist you to become aware of the things bothering you badly and into acknowledging all the aspects of life that provide you with more mental peace.**

DOPAMINE FASTING

Dopamine fasting is when you abstain from doing things that make you feel good in order to reset the released levels of the feel-good hormone which is dopamine.

Dopamine is a crucial neurotransmitter that is created within our brain. Dopamine is vital, as it helps to guide our emotions, motivation and experiences of pleasure.

I want you to be aware that the resetting of your brain's dopamine levels requires patience. It will take time, but you should begin at once to limit over-indulgence in activities that surge releases of dopamine; or simply do these activities with more balance.

As previously expressed, all things in life thrive better in balance and harmony, and this also applies to our daily pleasures and feel good activities.

If for the last 100 days you've done the same thing that releases dopamine, then by taking a short break from whatever it is you enjoy, you can reset the amounts of this feel-good hormone released when returning to doing such things. Think of it like this: would the theme park be as thrilling if you attended it every evening?

Absolutely not.

Of course, we get dopamine from daily doings and some of these aspects of life we can't avoid, but I believe there is no harm in actively attempting to abstain from excessive dopamine releases. You will get heightened enjoyment from the things you may have gotten used to doing. As with all things done often, we can end up becoming immune to them, so a short break can reinstate our levels of appreciation and enjoyment; quite literally giving more potent feelings of pleasure.

After doing the same thing for 100 days in a row you'll feel less impact from the release of dopamine because you would have become used to it. However, by fasting and abstaining from your enjoyments, you literally will enjoy them more upon returning to them or bringing more balance to how often you do them.

It's almost as if it is a life-hack that works by simply taking a break, thus increasing the chemicals' impact on you mentally. As with any other aspect of life, with a little bit of absence or abstinence, you will feel the difference. When you consistently do things that release dopamine, you get used to the hormones released. Try fasting from enjoyments for 7 days, and upon doing so you will have a new appreciation for the aspects of life you already enjoyed.

I have used dopamine fasting in my own life in regard to going to the gym. **I trained for years through my mental hardships because it provided me with positivity to counter-attack the negatives**. I was in need of the release of both serotonin and dopamine, but when going to the gym everyday, I began to feel its positive impacts less, so I opted to remove it from my daily routine. I did this in order to reset the feel-good hormones I received from my daily doings.

A week out of the gym will enable you to feel next week's endorphins of fitness with maximum effect; literally more potent happiness hormones all due to a week of abstinence. This is one aspect of life that I wish I was aware of sooner because I seem to never rest.

Dopamine fasting is something I have been practising for a while, and I genuinely thought of this idea myself with no external influence, but after years of putting this to practise, I have now come to find there are many studies in regard to it and its effects.

Dopamine fasting has worked very well for me personally over the last few years and has assisted me through some difficult times as it reset the levels of dopamine released while doing daily things, which enabled me to really enjoy all aspects of my life once again.

As we all know, fasting from food (although it's difficult) does come with health benefits. I believe dopamine fasting is such a good method for us to utilise to benefit our mental health, and by practising dopamine fasting, you will need to have a digital detox. The life many of us live these days consists of spending far too much time on social media and other digital platforms. Dopamine fasting is when you abstain from all things that release dopamine, so this means we will need to deprive ourselves of many of our feel-good aspects and enjoyments of life. Keep in mind, it's only for a short period of time to reinstate the feel-good impact of doing something you enjoy. This will consist of temporarily taking a break from things such as: exercising, all forms of technology, intimacy, habits such as drinking or smoking, and even from engaging in too many conversations. I do this at times when I wish to regain my mental balance, but also when I feel like an aspect of life I really enjoy doesn't feel as enjoyable anymore. When you begin to enjoy one of your forms of entertainment less, that could be the very signal you need to opt into a 7 day dopamine fast. That's how I notice when I need some deprivation of dopamine. **In life, as our own mental pilot, we need to pay close attention to signals of distress, and one of these signals could be enjoying what we usually enjoy substantially less!**

I am a strong believer that when we feel mental turbulence, it is as if we have an engine warning light that something in our lives needs altering, adding or removing.

I believe that we don't simply feel these ways for no reason, so when I begin to enjoy less what was once my favourite thing, I know empirically that this is my time to work on my ways of living. Otherwise, I won't enjoy the mental turbulence that comes with not fixing things. I am currently enrolling into a neuroscience course to further my understanding, but I have just completed a 13 assignment course on awareness of 12 different forms of mental illness/health.

I'm working toward increasing my knowledge in order to help and heal others. Dopamine fasting could be just what you need to regain mental balance, and as I write this very sentence, only just yesterday I decided to completely delete Snapchat. For many years I was recording my every moment or movement, and then I realised I had an attachment to capturing memories because I am very sentimental and due to the childhood difficulties I went through, I find it hard to piece the experiences into a timely order.

I don't know exactly when it began but I, as many others do started recording every moment, which literally takes away from the experience, because you're more focussed on a good recording than embracing what is actually happening. This led to me being more conscious of other people's envy. Even though I always walk in my shoes with confidence, video logging everything began to result in me portraying a life much better than I am genuinely living. It is important, as your own mental pilot, to analyse what is causing or increasing your difficulties. So follow in my footsteps with a step back from social media. For there is a worthwhile reward of removing unnecessary dosages of dopamine and to eliminating the far too much time we spend connected and focussed on our digital screens.

When in a prison cell with no phone, I had a chance to fully analyse my thoughts in silence. We have so many distractions surrounding us that this time also showed me how powerful our phones can be if utilised wisely. **I had a limited number of books with me in the cell, but with our cellphones we have infinite information right at our fingertips.** Unfortunately, instead of using these technologies to benefit us, we use them blindly and allow them to not always impact our lives in a positive way. Many of us do not realise the amount of distractions that digital platforms have on our lives. I've seen with my own two eyes how social media can leave a man's mental health in ruins. So with a dopamine detox, you shift yourself towards being more stable and focussed without overdosing on dopamine. Some critics of the concept of dopamine fasting say that it is not good to abstain from dopamine releases, as the neurotransmitters play a key role in everyday life.

YES, of course, it plays a massive role in everyday life but too much or too little dopamine has been linked to development of many mental disorders. It's important we strive towards balance and as our own mental pilots, it is our duty to do so. Always do what works right for you, because **some critics will be critical about something that could genuinely be of help to you** personally. Do actions that mentally alleviate you of any form of adversity. **Do not allow the opinions of others to impact your effort toward doing what results in your own mental comfort.** Sadly, in the cases of some of those beautiful souls who have lost their lives to suicide, one of the main causes for the saddest of happenings was because they cared too much to please everyone and gave too much power and importance to the opinions of others. Do not fly in turbulence just to be perceived as perfect by others. Instead, as long as you ain't harming anyone else, do your own thing and whatever it is you need to do in order to get you through and then beyond your struggles.

As I previously discussed, everything in life requires balance. By limiting dopamine releases, you will actually be avoiding impulsive, addictive and aggressive behaviours.

Many medical studies relate dopamine deficiency to a number of disorders such as:

Attention Deficit Hyperactivity Disorder(ADHD), Schizophrenia and depression.

Excessive dopamine levels, according to medical studies suggest that you may have increased aggression, increased experiences of impulsive behaviour, ADHD and an increase in symptoms of an addictive personality.

If we can abstain from the things that make us feel good we will develop a heightened sense of self control, because if we can withstand from what feels best, then we will definitely develop the strength to stop what's detrimental to us. So, you can view dopamine fasting not only as a positive reset in the brain's release of the feel-good hormone, but also as a challenge to build up your own mental strength, discipline and self control.

The forms of fasting spiritually and religiously are not just based around not eating. We are taught by our religious and spiritual teachers that we need to lower our gazes, limit our listening to music (as the lyrics are more often than not prohibited), connect to our inner spirit, and to avoid anything explicit. Many people oversee the true depths of their fasting by thinking it's completely food based. We are taught to fast from our pleasures alongside our abstinence from food and water, and in doing so we feel more connected to god in our spirits. Even as an atheist, your thoughts will be much clearer and the great dopamine reset will enhance our feel-good feelings.

After a break from all the things that make me feel good, when I do them again the dopamine release feels much more noticeable and this leads me to feel more happy and content. When you have an imbalance of dopamine, at times nothing you are doing feels good enough.

This applies to a break from physical exercise as well. Serotonin releases are so pivotal in regard to the maintenance of my mental health that the gym is a task I attempt to pilot into a daily doing. However, upon taking a short break from the gym, I miss the antidote to depression (which is serotonin), and when I return to my sanctuary of any form of training, I literally can't stop the feeling of being very happy. This is exactly how after going to the gym, even if it is raining heavily, I walk home happily through each raindrop. It's all due to the natural chemicals released within my body, which guides me into being mentally so much more positive and physically so much stronger.

It is factual in my experiences that physical exercise quite literally conquers my mental turbulence.
You will develop more self control and discipline with purposeful abstinence from the aspects of life that release dopamine. This may sound like an easy task, but it may be just as difficult for some, as it is to be fasting for long hours and smelling food cooking. Many of us have an addiction to quick releases of dopamine, **such as continuously flicking through Instagram. This is exactly how we develop shorter attention spans, but** with time away from such dopamine stimulations, we can reconnect with our inner self. We will begin to gain more understanding of ourselves and we will feel our best while becoming our best version.
I don't see any negatives in regard to having a **digital detox.** As I'm writing this, only just 2 days ago, I have made the decision that for the whole month of March, I'm removing myself from being on social media everyday. With this simple decision I know for a fact that I have just gained an extra 1 or 2 hours of time daily to be utilised on more important things; such as getting this very book closer to completion and true physical and mental improvement. All while cleansing my consciousness from seeing all the different forms of unpredictable posts, which we see daily on social media at any given moment.
The very least we can do is ensure that we follow accounts with positive content because the worst news always spreads the quickest and the positive posts don't always receive the support they deserve. I know this first hand through raising awareness and money for charity. I posted real-life videos of the kids in the Ugandan orphanage that were in need of help. It never got reposted much, but I'm forever grateful for the money I did gather to help those in Africa. Yet on social media I see people reposting many negative occurrences with no hesitation.

A detox from these platforms will do you no harm. Many individuals convince themselves, myself included, that we need social media interactions to become a success. However, the reality is what is always shown will eventually lose attention and by taking time away from social platforms it will increase people's interest. It's good to keep people updated but not when it's costing you a bag full of energy that could be used for genuine progress.

Pause. If I spent less time on those platforms, my book could've already been finished.

I'm not completely against social media; I'm actually a fan, but it absolutely needs to be limited to a place and time. There is not much worse for your morning routine than waking up and going straight onto Instagram. Do not do actions that pollute your days and as your own mental pilot it's good to try out new ways to live.

If at times you feel like you aren't enjoying the aspects of life you used to, then a dopamine fast could be exactly what you require.

Dopamine fasting is not much different from the religious and spiritual forms of abstaining from life's indulgences. It's difficult to not eat food or drink water for a certain amount of hours, but let's see how difficult it will be to avoid spending time on the many forms of social media during this period. These social apps provide us with short shots of dopamine which is what makes them so addictive. It's one shot of dopamine after the other in quick succession. Spending time on these apps quite literally damages our attention spans, and not only that, they are literally **DIGITAL DRUGS.** These massive platforms will be the cause of many disturbing developments in the human brain and I for one don't want to begin to imagine where and how far it may take us away from actually being a human being. It's reported that on average, each user spends approximately 1 hour on these apps a day, some more or less, but do the calculation over the course of a year of *how much time we spend on these apps that could be the exact cause of our mental detriment.* If you spend an hour a day, that's 15 days a year, half a month yearly in total, which you have spent on these platforms that could very well be the cause of your mental turbulence. Just the same way you run a trial on the new things you try, we will need to run a trial on how we feel mentally after the removal of certain aspects or doings in our lives. Think of it as your own mental renovation and by the end of it you will be your own best version.

Another reason why fasting from your usual sources of dopamine is good, is that depending on the type of fasting you're doing, it could also help assist you in trying new things. This works well with the next chapter, **passion pursuit,** because when you're taking a break from the aspects of life that provide you with the feel-good hormone, you instantly gain more time to try new things in the process. As with my example about taking a break from the gym; let's say I go to gym around 2 hours a day, and then on the week I'm dopamine fasting, I gain 2 hours a day to try new things. That's 14 hours across the week and that's only the calculation of gym-going. So on your dopamine fasting weeks you can actually find a passion you have been pursuing or you can use those free hours to put more effort into achieving your goals and targets.

Depriving yourself from certain aspects of life can enable you to massively appreciate them. I know one person who wasn't conscious of time and didn't see his kids often, but after his prison sentence he realised that life had such a deeper meaning and now after having to wait on 2 weekend visits a month to see his son, he tries his utmost best to keep in good spirits with his child's mother so he can spend as much time with his son as possible now that he's home. Although this situation is hopefully something none of you will ever have to experience, prison can teach you to appreciate some parts of life you may have once severely overlooked. That means depriving yourself from some of your feel-good aspects of life will most definitely remind and reinstall your conscious appreciation for the life you do have.

Now you are aware. Congratulations on becoming your very own MENTAL PILOT.

As you are improving,
And you are improving,
You'll begin to notice.

Artwork by Annalise B.

3
PASSION PURSUIT

I believe having a passion is one of the most important and pivotal parts of maintaining a happy, healthy and positive lifestyle.

There is so much more to you than you will ever know; you literally can gain a skill set in anything you practise.

I dislike when I hear an individual state that they can't do something...

Yeah, well we all once couldn't walk but we crawled and fell many times learning how to and then through persistence and repetition we conquered the challenge of what we once couldn't do but now find natural. So **never say you can't, just state that you haven't persistently attempted to**. We will always be unaware of our true capabilities because humans can perform miracles when persistently practising the extraordinary.

Do things your own way, be a **TRAILBLAZER!**

Don't seek approval from others when pursuing your passion, even if you do things very differently from others, it's your own unique way of doing things. Imagine this:

If one crab learned to crawl straight on a beach full of left to right crawling crabs, **he would be disapproved of for his differences**, but those very differences are actually more efficient. Do things your own way and don't be shy to locate a passion which is different, as it will lead to a whole new skill set.

This expresses the importance of discovering a passion that resonates with you.

Don't just do what everyone else is doing because your hidden talent may be in a passion that's different from your family and friendship group.

Ask yourself, are you truly enjoying what you do?

Or are you enjoying the company you do it with?

I want you to realise the reality that your passion could be something you would've never predicted.

The impatient man could actually find that he enjoys fishing.

The lady who is shy could actually be a natural in front of the camera for modelling.

The person who has never physically exercised in their life could find they enjoy weightlifting.

Passion pursuit is a great way to find a new hobby, but it is also effective at finding a secret talent.

I have a question..

How would an amazing singer ever have become aware of their amazing voice if they hadn't ever sung?

How would the boxing world champion find out their expertise in the ring without having to try boxing for the first time?

It's important you try new things. Everything you are now comfortable with was once a first try. We have no excuse to not try something new. Many activities offer a free first day trial class to test if it's something you're interested in. **Don't just do what is popular to do.** Be receptive, find your own calling card, and it may well end up as a business path or a sports career.

We don't realise it, but sports are limited to certain places and classes of people.

For example:

Cricket is one of the sports that Englanders are very talented at and excel in, but coming from a council estate in London, I can wholeheartedly say I don't know a single cricket player or even a tennis player. That's the god's honest truth. So my question is... how many people from within these sport-limited places, who deeply love both football and boxing, could've been world class at cricket or tennis?

Could you imagine if the favelas of Brazil weren't visited by football scouts?

So many of the world's best footballers would've never been found. So, this chapter is going to be about you, finding yourself, and your hobbies that can lead to secret skills.

Funny enough, only just recently a famous British cricket player started a project to bring cricket into the less-fortunate places in England and by doing so found many young kids who were extremely talented at cricket. Kids who would've never played it had the project not taken place...

As I will mention in the chapter '**Consciousness**', by becoming more aware, you expand your reality and thus can make your reality expand. One such way is by trying and developing new skills through hobbies and passions.

Passion Pursuit is a great way to shake up your life and learn new things. At the end of the pursuit you can select your favourite hobbies and apply them to your lifestyle.

Passion Pursuit isn't just sports related, as I have tried numerous new things during my pursuit, including reading, painting, writing, making music, cycling, fishing, snooker, museum visits, long walks in nature, and even yoga.

I suggest listening to one random song from any genre everyday and I bet you'll find a song you like which you would've never usually listened to.

Many times in life when people have free time and have no passions to follow, this is when they do something that doesn't benefit them. So, finding a passion that will keep you focussed, fit, and happy is actually very important.

Once passions are found, you will never again feel boredom. I only express advice that I, myself, have practised and applied to my life,

"Practise what you preach but only preach what you have practised"-Sean Atlas Walsh

The purpose of this chapter is to give you a push towards discovering something that stimulates your body, mind, and soul.

What if your life's true passions ignite and begin at the end of your comfort zone?

What if the instrument you have never tried is the exact instrument that you can naturally play so fluently?

What if the sport you have never had the courage to try is the sport that you are insanely gifted at?

Many individuals inherit the passions of their parents, and this is why it's crucial to Passion Pursuit, because you will find something that resonates with you. Try everything you want to, for there is nothing to lose, and in your pursuit who knows where it may lead you.

There is no limit to the potential of your skillset when passion pursuing.

You can look back at your childhood to locate, then restart a forgotten passion, or look forward to trying multiple new things; as both options are exciting.

If you do begin playing a sport you once played, even if only just one day a week, that means you have that one day to look forward to each week that is healthy for you and gives you the opportunity to make new friends as well when joining a team. You will have more socialising chances with people of different backgrounds and you will be getting stronger whilst playing a sport you used to enjoy in your younger years.

My older sister joined a netball team more than 14 years after she last played and guess what? **To no surprise, she enjoyed it just as much as she used to in her younger years.**

In your pursuit of a passion, it doesn't need to be a new discovery, as it could be something that you have stopped doing or something you have actually missed doing. Get back to being the more passionate version of yourself because you will not only be experiencing joy and maintaining your happiness, but you will also be developing positive characteristics. You will develop new skills, but these positive characteristics already exist deep within you. It's up to you to come out of your shell and do the things that you love doing, which in turn, will allow these characteristics to shine through.

Passionate people are individuals who are focussed on what *can* be, rather than what actually *is*. They enjoy the journey; not just the final outcome or destination.

Passionate individuals have an unwavering belief that they will achieve what they passionately set their mind to.

People who are passionate look forward to doing the task they love as if it is a special event. I'm passionate about this book and I promise you that writing this doesn't feel like work at all. As a result of doing what you're passionate about, you will have increased effort, willingness, optimism and performance; which are all great characteristics to have and are simply a consequence of partaking in your passions. **As you uncover these strong traits you have within, hard**

work and life gets that little bit easier, and you will face less adversity.

LESS ADVERSE

Passions will limit the difficulties of the task you are doing. The difficulty will be less daunting and impactful, and what I mean by this is, when you do something you don't enjoy, one hour could feel like three hours. However, **upon doing something you are passionate about, the hours can speed past without you even noticing**.

The difficulty of what you are doing is limited. I'll give you a personal example:

When I run on a treadmill, after 15 minutes I'm already fatigued…

But drop me on a football pitch and somehow I'm increasingly more fit. **Passions can remove psychological difficulty.**

Passions that you can utilise to comfort you during hardships are very important, as they will limit your mental adversity during times of difficulty, and I know this from firsthand experience.

If you are ever in doubt regarding the impact passions can have on your standard of life, explain to me how a disabled person's quality of life can be massively uplifted due to them being passionate about music?

I have a very close friend who sadly had an accident and is now disabled but is slowly recovering. My friend, Meshach, has a passion for making beats and when he's in his creative mode it's like he's in another universe. This is due to his passion for music-making, during which his spirit gets so uplifted.

I met a man once who was disabled and unable to walk, and he expressed to me that when music is playing it makes him feel like he is moving. In that very moment I

realised although he isn't physically moving, his soul is absolutely dancing!

Passions will assist you through adversity, I promise you.

I preach this so loudly because I have used my passions to alleviate the adverse stressful situations I have been in. I will never doubt the impacts a passion can have on an individual. Whether that be stress on the road to success, or the more sad happenings in life such as the loss of a loved one, passions will help you to overcome the hardships.

After the passions are of aid to you, you will be even more passionate about them.

Imagine this, I saw my dad's dead body on the 19th of May 2008. My family is so passionate about Manchester United and guess who won the biggest trophy in football club competition on the 21st of May 2008…

MANCHESTER UNITED.

Two days after my dad's death, we were champions of Europe, and that provided me with happiness because I was cheering that win for him whilst crying.

I wrote a poem yesterday sitting in the graveyard next to my dad's headstone. I didn't plan to but it just happened. It was the first time I shed teardrops over my handwriting, but my passion for writing helped me express myself and feel good in that moment. When visiting my father's grave, I looked to the sky and comprehended the lives many of us are living.

We all need to truly live before we die and for me, when I'm spending time in the aspects of life I'm passionate about, that's exactly when I feel most alive.

New passions lead to new heights.

You can use these passions to help you reduce stress, use them to release some physical energy, or even to just give you a break from reality. I used football to give me that much needed break from reality to recharge.

My passion for football even helped me get over the death of my father.

Still to this day, whenever I play, I get an instant sanctuary. That's because all my focus is on the pitch in which I play. **A break from our own thoughts is sometimes all we need to recharge**.

A couple days after my father passed away, we went to visit the funeral parlour to see him one last time and I was holding my father's head in my hands, knowing it would be the last time I would ever see him.

I was beyond upset, but even during such trauma and loss, simply stepping onto the pitch to play football took me away from all thoughts and emotion. It's like when I was on the pitch I took a break from earth and all it's troubles.

It's truly a Win-Win Situation, because I got more fit from all the running as I was also mentally de-stressing.

I still use this method today during all forms of stress I experience, whether it is work-related or personal annoyances. I hit the gym and attack the iron, which clears my thoughts, conquers my anger, and relieves me of all stress; all while making me physically stronger.

Win-Win Situation.

"Inner demons do not enjoy it when you are exercising… You wouldn't remain around those who do actions you don't like… neither will those inner demons, so do exactly what they don't like and exercise!

You will feel so much better mentally, physically and spiritually when becoming passionate about exercising. I'm preaching this because I have practised it and I've felt its full effects.

When doing an exercise you enjoy, you will burn calories with less mental struggle, thus making the physical task less difficult.

Ask yourself, **how did the obese man lose all that weight after having his heart break?**

He found comfort with a new-found passion for exercising.

I say **when**, because we all will at some stage, **when** we are overthinking we need to channel our focus into something, otherwise our thoughts will run wild and freely and for many people this is exactly when they begin to think negatively.

A passion doesn't only provide you with entertainment and comfort. It will also provide you with focus, so you can utilise your passions when overthinking.

If you find yourself overthinking, which I do often due to living alone and away from family since 14 years old,

I use reading a book to stop my mind running wild with thought. This is also a

Win-Win Situation because **you cancel negative overthinking whilst increasing knowledge by reading**.

When your thoughts begin to run wild, that's the very moment you need to guide your thoughts back into focus. Don't forget you are still your own *mental pilot*, and hindering overthinking by book-reading means you will be preventing mental turbulence.

Some individuals will look back on their past and realise that they spent time with the wrong people just to provide them with comfort from their own thoughts. I wish I discovered reading as a hobby of mine sooner, because it's something I really enjoy that I didn't expect, and reading interlinks with my lifestyle very well due to the majority of my other passions including physical activity. So reading is the passion I make use of when resting and recovering, and yet it still stimulates my mind. Finding a passion for something will mean you can rely upon yourself when things go bad or negative.

If you as my reader can think of any other win-win counterattacks of stress; feel free to get in touch, as we can all learn from one another.

Facebook has a hobbies section if you require some inspiration for new things to do for your fitness and entertainment.

Social media is so good at making me aware of unusual upcoming events. Only 2 weeks ago, I noticed an advert for an event that is taking place on my birthday weekend. Now, me and my friends have booked tickets and we are literally going to be partying on the beach for my birthday.

There is no limit to the forms of entertainment suggested, which could then become something you are passionate about. It's good to try something new because you may enjoy something unpredictable.

Jazz cafes in London with cheap entry and good energy. Comedy shows in small bars nearby in the city.

Even gatherings for lectures discussing many forms of fascinating study.There is so much more to try and experience within your own city. There are new things to try all around us. There are many new places to see, so **become a tourist of your own town**, and I guarantee you there is more to your community than you are aware of. Go out and pursue something new!

Boredom can push you into finding something new. I had my nephew over for a sleepover and I didn't want him playing video games excessively. He eventually got bored of colouring, then all of a sudden he found a way to climb onto my pull-up bar...

Now, he's only 5 years old, but I know that he will always have a passion for one of the best strength-gaining exercises one could ever do; all due to boredom increasing his curiosity.

Don't always look for easy distractions because true boredom may lead you to do something unpredictably positive.

You can find a passion by being spontaneous and trying many new things. My little sister, Siobhan, and I went for food to have a catch-up and then on our way home we stopped off at a shop that sold numerous different things. Spontaneously I purchased flower seeds for my sister and I randomly set a challenge for her to grow some flowers and who knows…

She may end up developing a new-found passion for gardening, which I wouldn't be surprised about either, because my little sister is spiritual and enjoys manifesting things, which I believe is all interlinked. We grow as people just as the plants do, and we need to plant seeds of improvement and manifest brighter days.

Humans, animals and plants are all living things and we are all a part of nature.

Tree-huggers aren't insane at all, it is scientifically proven that trees have energy fields and are full of energy. Their roots go deep into the soil upon which we walk.

Research has proven there are real benefits to be derived from tree-hugging. It sounds funny right?

This further shows that whatever you want to do, no matter how it is perceived by others, you should do it as long as it's beneficial to you and your well-being.

Time in nature benefits us in many ways, such as:

Reducing our stress, improving our immunity, lowering blood pressure and calming our anxieties.

If you ever feel really anxious about anything, take a walk in the woods, along the river, or even walk peacefully through the busy city. You will feel alleviated of your stress and your anxieties will gradually decrease.

You only need to visit the forest once to feel mentally refreshed from my personal experience, so with the scientific backing to prove there are benefits from tree-hugging, would you have the courage to do it even if it is viewed as weird by others?

Do not let opinions of others halt you from trying new things, because you will be allowing others' opinions to hinder you from locating and loving a new passion.

As I write this, I just purchased a book called *The Hidden Life of Trees* by Peter Wohlleben. I believe after reading this book, the forest will become more magical to everyone, even those who are sceptical.

Hugging a tree isn't that weird. After all, if a human's hug can comfort you when you are sad, then a tree's hug could regenerate the energy within you.

The Western world highly respects the teachings and spiritual guidance we receive from the Far East... whether that be religious or just to connect to our spirits.

There is a Japanese practice called 'Shinrin Yoku' (森林浴) which is translated into 'Forest Bathing.' This practice is about gaining spiritual, physical and psychological benefits from reconnecting to nature; meaning reconnecting to ourselves.

If you have a passion for something that most people may find odd, it doesn't matter what they think, because that very passion provides you with focus, entertainment, comfort and can lead to pathways of income.

For example: take plane and train spotters. I don't know one person who does this, but that doesn't mean it's unable to provide those who do it with happiness or maybe even income via photography.

Always follow through on anything you feel could potentially be a passion for you.

It is essential to have hobbies which are sensible and of positive impact. This is so pivotal towards maintaining ourselves because we all know life can get difficult at times, and when these hard times affect those who have no positive means of coping or passions to turn to, people often end up turning to the wrong coping mechanisms; such as substance abuse. These will lead to an overall downward spiral, so learn from the mistakes of those before you.

As you're on the Passion Pursuit you'll get to know yourself better empirically.

You may be surprised with your new-found capabilities, so what's stopping you from trying something new?

There are so many different hobbies available; all offering introduction classes to see if it's something of interest to you or not. There's nothing to lose, but there is a whole world of passions to discover and potentially love.

An example of how you can utilise these free introduction classes is to try the 3 closest gyms to your house. Do all one-day introductions to see which atmosphere you feel the most comfortable with and that matches your needs. The closest gym to you may not be the one for you, so don't give up on potential passions due to one bad experience at one place.

I once swapped the gym I was going to simply to another gym that was literally on the opposite side of the road, and it impacted my commitment and mood to train massively in a positive way.

I want you to acknowledge that it is factual that you *have* and *can* develop many forms of skills you don't even know about because, as I mentioned, with the amazing singer only knowing of their voice after having sung; it's the same way you still have many skills unknown to yourself…

"Do not fish in a pond if you have the ability to fish in the sea. Do not limit your own possibilities by not using your abilities."-Sean Walsh

SELF CARE

You may need to be selfish in the most kind way possible because this is about **you**. It's about giving **yourself** a real chance to try and enjoy new things, and who knows where you may end up?

I want you to remember this as you are on your pursuit of passions; that the more things you try that aren't for you, the closer you will be to discovering what is.

"As with a bunch of keys, each time you try the wrong key, you get closer to finding the key that will unlock the door. So with trying new hobbies, each hobby that you discover isn't for you, brings you closer to the hobby that is; which will then become a passion of yours."-Sean Walsh

Be passionate about self care!

Some individuals have more passion for taking care of their cars than their own physical health. Try to comprehend that. We need to act now towards developing a passion for self care. There are many forms of self care; every small action that is to aid, heal or improve you is self care. You will feel so much better mentally, physically and spiritually by being passionate about looking after yourself. These days many people are more concerned with the materialistic aspects of life, to the point where they're beginning to lose sight of what's really important.

Of course nice clothing is stylish and can have an impact on our moods while wearing them, but **what about your well-being deep within?** Isn't that of much more importance? The majority of people will choose to be genuinely healthier in their bodies, rather than to look good on their exteriors, so why do people put more attention into what they're going to be wearing rather than improving how they feel within?

This is exactly why I make sure I take action leading up to an important day to feel mentally positive, more than focusing on how I look or how I dress.

Someone can look a million pounds but feel internally depressed and I'd rather feel my best and look average.

There are many forms of taking care of ourselves. Self care is stretching your muscles. Self care is putting cream on your skin. Self care is every little thing you can think of that is of benefit to your existence. Be passionate in taking good care of yourself and you will feel a massive improvement in your overall well-being.

I have a question...

Why not take yourself to the cinema?

Why do you need others to be with you to do things that you enjoy?

Two years ago I spontaneously went to the cinema alone and guess what? I had a good time doing so.

We should never need others to be with us for us to do the things in life we enjoy.

My friend Sanchez took himself on holiday and to no surprise he had an amazing time and even extended his stay!

Do not be shy to self-entertain; you don't need others with you to be self caring.

Once you begin to look after yourself, you will realise that it is an expression of self love. This isn't arrogance, it is more of a passion of who you are and having positive pride in taking care of yourself.

Our very creation is a true blessing. If you are a believer of God, it means that your body was created by the most high, so how can you not take care of the gift of life that has been blessed upon you? Even if you are a non-believer of God, take a second to contemplate that your very existence was against all the odds in a vast universe, but here we are all existing on a beautiful planet, so be passionate about your own existence by partaking in self care.

Self care is also actively taking action towards putting to practise the methods you hear myself and others preaching. That's because by **reading them and not taking action, not much will transform**. Miracles do happen, but they're highly rare, and it's better to just actively push for self-development than to wait for a situation in which you change in an instant. Gradual progression is better than no progress at all.

By partaking in true self care you could end up extending your lifespan. Daily vitamins and daily absolutely anything that aids you towards being a healthier version can increase your lifespan.

No one has ever regretted being self caring, but many have been regretful of not taking more care of themselves when health issues do arise.

There is no good in accumulating wealth whilst losing health. A financially **poor person who has health is richer than the millionaire who is ill**. This is why it's crucial that you become passionate in regard to self care, as it will enhance your health.

Passion & **Paycheques**

"Passions lead to pathways of income…
Follow your passions first and then you'll make money doing what you love."-SeanAtlasWalsh

Many career paths and lifetime passions come from the first try of a new hobby, task, or challenge. So enjoy your passion pursuit and grow into the new-found passionate you.

If you want to live happily whilst earning money, make sure you get a job doing what you have love and passion for. **Don't allow the paycheque** to tempt you away from doing what you want to do. If you do allow the pay to influence your decision on such an important part of life, then you will have to **pay the price of spending your time and effort working a daunting job you don't enjoy.**

I will elaborate more in a later chapter about how we need to actively attempt to never feel regrets and **one of the biggest regrets you will feel in later-life will be the years you ignored your passions due to paycheque chasing.**

It is true that it isn't always possible to do everything you enjoy when making money, and this is why I aim for 80% of my time being spent on what I want to do, including work... And then 20% of my time is spent on sorting out the parts of life I don't want to be doing.

I believe it's important to target this way of living or else you will most likely end up spending it the other way around, which none of us would want. This is exactly why it's pivotal that you pursue a passion, because you will develop a skill that you could earn from, or teach others and be paid for.

In life, if you are solely concerned about money-making, it is highly likely you will not do the things you are passionate about, unless of course your passion is to chase financial freedom. as then you'll be content with the forms of income you're making regardless. Still, you'll need to pursue a passion to ignite your creative side or to entertain and comfort you. Of course we need to make money to survive but trust me that if you leap towards attempting to get paid for your passions, you will never fall short because you'll be much happier on a daily basis. I often ask people:

Does the increase in salary doing what you don't love compensate for the mental suffering you feel on a daily basis?

Doing a job you hate just because of the pay means everyday you will want to be anywhere else other than where you are.

So receiving less pay, but doing what you love, will result in you feeling much happier.

If you always chase the paycheques whilst ignoring your passions, then you will end up feeling **despondent**. Google defines this as:

"In low spirits from a loss of hope and courage."

Never solely chase the paycheque, because you'll end up spending the majority of your life doing what you don't want to be doing. Life is far too short to do such a thing, but of course money needs to be made. It's true, but earn it doing what you love doing, even if it is less than the pay of the job you hate. You will be rewarded by feeling more happy everyday.

Ask yourself within, are you happy doing what you're doing? Or do you feel like **the passion you have kept pushing to the side is now deserving of the chance to enlighten your life?**

This could set you on the path of living the life you want to live, earning money doing what you enjoy doing, and that sounds good right? But remember, as I said with self care, nothing will happen unless you take action to make it happen. How does a home go from untidy to clean? With **active effort**. So you want to go from unhappy and fed up of the life you have been living? Then it takes active effort to change your circumstances. Give yourself a chance; I believe you'll never end up regretting giving yourself a chance at this new path because even if it doesn't go completely to plan, you can always say wholeheartedly you gave yourself a try.

As with my analogy of the bunch of keys, with passion pursuing, view it as dating. You may find the one for you instantly or not be so lucky to find the right one in multiple attempts, but you won't give up on continuing to try. Don't give up, keep giving a chance to a new passion as if you've met a new person and eventually you will have located just what is for you.

A passion will ignite and change your life for the better just like when you find your soulmate.

Do not allow money to interfere with your passion pursuit. You wouldn't leave someone who is good for you for someone else who is of detriment, but richer in finances, would you?

Don't allow money to hold you back from being passionate, as many of us in our adult years do.

The truth is, you have a passion within that will develop your skills and result in avenues of income. So do not allow any exterior influences to affect the possibility of you discovering and developing what's already within you. It's not quite a leap of faith, because you will be shifting towards a better, healthier, happier and more flourishing life. Not only that, passion will provide you with refuge during times of turmoil. Without my passions supplying me with entertainment, focus, purpose and deeper understanding of myself, who knows what I could've turned to instead?

Who knows who I would've become without them? One thing I know for sure is that I wouldn't be in a better position than I am currently in.

HAPPY PASSION PURSUIT

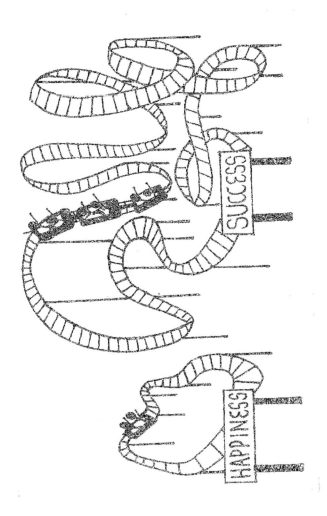

Artwork by Annalise B.

4

THE MIDDLE MARATHON

The middle marathon is when you are in the middle stage of progression on your chosen path and you feel not much is taking place. Things may have slowed down or you may even be facing some middle stage difficulty.

It is important that you keep in mind that **nothing worth having comes easy,** so when facing obstacles whilst pursuing your ambitions, don't get disheartened or lose focus because the obstacles could be signs that you're giving your utmost best and that you are well on route to making progress.

Overworking can be difficult and you may also feel like you're losing yourself at intervals due to lack of time to do the things you want to do or even to simply have time to rest and relax. However, it's important you **find comfort in the hard work** required to achieve what you set out to do. You can find more comfort in working hard when becoming aware that both working and not working have their fair share of struggles. To be overworked and tired still lands you with a feeling of purpose, progression and financial income.

On the other hand, being unemployed can result in an individual feeling like they have no benefit to the community, unemployment can increase a person's laziness and this also results in other mental adversities such as lack of self confidence and depression; not to mention the lower quality of life you'll live with more money problems.

I'd much prefer to work hard and then enjoy the fruits of my labour overseas on a beach, than to endure the difficulties those unemployed face while remaining in the same city and in the same situation; without much happening at all.

In life, people often look at others' scenarios and compare their situation to their own. You shouldn't do this because **to every painting there's more than just a splash of colours**, you don't see all the time, skill, and commitment invested for a person to become successful by viewing their current version. People sacrifice so much on their own path to success that you should never compare your lifestyle to anyone else's, for this could leave you feeling less motivated. Especially **on social media, because people mostly only show their good side and you then begin to compare your adversities to what seems to be others' ease. This will be of massive detriment to your motivation.** In the middle marathon we need to attempt to make everything easier to cope with and not decrease our motivation.

There are difficulties to both being overworked and not working at all, so what type of difficulty would you prefer to face?

I'll choose the hard work!

In life we need to stop viewing our difficulties as unique, as everyone experiences hardship but some allow the pain to consume them and others learn to use that pain as fuel for progress.

Do not inherit a victim-mentality because the reality is the turmoil you've gone through or still endure could be the reason you actually succeed.

If you don't have parental support or any other form of safety nets in the process of doing what you desire, do not get discouraged, for having no safety nets or people to rely on could be the exact scenario you need to force yourself to succeed.

Utilise your time more wisely, spend it on preparing yourself and taking action regarding the things you can control, instead of wasting energy on negative situations you can't control. As we all know, overthinking will have us envisioning negative occurrences, which more than likely will never happen. We could overthink 100 possible outcomes and even then the outcome could be different to anything we envisioned.

The middle marathon is about how to assist ourselves in decreasing difficulty on the pathway of improvement, well... Communication is pivotal towards getting through and beyond difficulties and this applies to all aspects of our lives, both relationship and work-based.

Do not only focus on the problems you are facing, for some of these problems may simply be a result of bad or lack of communication. Focus on improving the communication amongst yourself and others and some of the problems will begin to dissolve.

Many couples go around in circles attempting to fix their issues in the relationship when **it isn't the problems themselves that need rectifying, it is the communication that needs fine tuning.** The same happens in workplace environments: problems arise by a lack of clear communication and this results in lack of understanding. **An improvement in quality of communication can remove all potential misunderstandings.**

Disagreements will ultimately increase your understanding of a situation and help you notice where communication can be worked on and improved. If you keep this positive outlook then you will experience less annoyance and anger. Why hold onto resentment when a simple conversation can deepen your understanding and remove bad emotions? Far too many individuals allow misunderstandings to cause them difficulties. 100% of the time it is wiser to converse with one another to increase understanding than to continue to hold onto negative emotions surrounding the issues that stem from bad communication.

NOT EASY

The aspects of life that aren't easy to obtain or to complete are more often than not the things in life that are better for you, so don't stop doing something because it isn't easy. If you always choose the easy option, it's likely you will not be making much progress. I say rest is a part of progress but I will never choose to do something just because it is easier. Do not allow the difficulty of a task to push you away from gaining its gain. It isn't easy, but that is exactly how it is supposed to be. Most easier options in life either increase our laziness or isn't a healthy option. **Through difficulties come the greatest of gains.**

Sometimes in life the only way through is to endure the difficulty or to remain in the same place, so don't always expect ease on your pathway to better circumstances, because at times there will be no easy option and to be honest **the adversity to obtain your achievements is what gives your success it's respect and honour.** Never view difficulty solely as a negative because **you can't praise a person for their resilience to not quit if they haven't been through adverse situations.**

All the difficulties will be worth enduring in the long run because you will have increased health, a stronger spirit and your financial circumstances will flourish with a characteristic of persevering through difficulties.

We sometimes impact our motivation negatively and that will always increase our difficulties. Losing weight isn't easy, but don't increase the difficulty or terminate your motivation by keeping a close eye on the numbers that the scales present. **The scales can be your enemy.** I have seen too many people quit their fitness journey because the scale doesn't seem to change regardless of their hard work and efforts.

I constantly hear, " I still weigh the same" or "how do I weigh more when I look slimmer?"

I'll tell you exactly why this is, because the composition of muscle and fat is different.

Let's say you have equally 5kg of both fat and muscle, the muscle would take up much less physical space than the fat and this explains why the scales can become your enemy. **You could be making so much physical improvement, gaining muscle whilst losing fat, and still weigh the same on the scales if not even heavier.**

You could be slim and muscular and weigh more than the person who is double your size physically and this is because muscle has high density.

Do not allow the numbers on the scales to decrease your work rate.

You don't have to look any further than combat sports to see a visualisation of the hardworking individuals, both men and women, being rewarded. Trading leather for a living isn't easy and it is exactly what brings these modern day warriors to their knees in tears when they get the gold strap and their name etched in history.

UFC fighters falling to their knees with tears, you know why? Pushing past every single day of difficulty, it isn't easy, but so much perseverance, hard work, pain, and suffering has been endured to get to that very moment. Not to mention how much they needed to sacrifice.

In life, most of us won't be physically dodging fists on the road to success, but life will attempt to knock you down with the hardships and obstacles we all face at different stages. After picking yourself up and persevering through, you will become successful and **it will feel so much sweeter than if it was easier**. Push on through everything life throws at you and you will always be proud of yourself. Only when someone quits can you truly say they have failed, and even then, what if they have quit one thing to succeed at something else?

> **"Do not make the same mistakes repetitively! Fail in different ways, then you will eventually find the way to succeed."**
> -Sean Atlas Walsh

It's also important we give 100% effort to our initial plans, because if we begin to plan our reaction to failure, then we take away energy from succeeding with plan A. It's good to have safety nets so you don't fall and fail in a way in which you can't bounce back.

It's perfectly fine to fail on your way to success, so don't completely change your initial plans due to some adversity or failures. Fail in different ways and then you will eventually find the way to formulate success.

Keep pushing forward and when you get past the middle stage difficulties, you will begin to cruise towards living the life you want to live because you have earned and created your success through perseverance, patience and organic methods.

Instead of dwelling on the difficulties, put active effort into pushing through obstacles, making progression and **never forget the importance of sacrifices in the process of elevation.**

Progression pain is a real thing. **Success requires sacrifice** and sacrifices aren't easy; although they aren't always noticed as one of the most important things to do for progress, they are crucial towards a better future. The two people that are equally talented will be separated by who is making the most sacrifices.

On your pathway to success you will experience all different forms of difficulty and sacrificing isn't easy, but you can use the 3 ways I will mention to keep you motivated, in a good position, and ready for the next step.

Don't count your struggles, notice your blessings!

Organically

You can let these middle stage difficulties play out organically and let nature take its course to show you the next best step on route to getting through middle marathon difficulty. This is the complete opposite of forcing things to happen and making hasty decisions. Liken this to 'going with the flow' or 'rolling with the punches.' By doing this you can actually be guided in a positive direction which you, yourself, couldn't have envisioned.

This will lead you in a direction that will present itself to make sense, for before you make a decision, things would've developed organically to show you what's best to do next. There is a practice done by doctors observing those with many forms of mental disorders and it is called **watchful waiting.** Watchful waiting is when you give some time, advisedly 2 weeks, to observe how things develop. This is normally used when treating someone with mental adversities but we can use **watchful waiting** in our lives to analyse what the best next step is to take and this is an organic way of moving forward, as it isn't forced at all.

I feel like letting things organically shape themselves is a smart tactic to use, because at times forcing progress actually does the complete opposite and can ruin your chances of making the right decisions in the midst of middle marathon adversity.

It is far better to maintain yourself through difficulties and then let things organically grow in the best direction.

It is likely in 2 weeks you will feel better surrounding a situation and you will know the best action to take, without having to force it.

"When things are forced, they are less authentic."
By letting your struggles organically pass and/or heal, you won't make bad decisions leading to more obstacles.

When animals are injected with chemicals to accelerate their growth, the taste is affected massively. When eggs are organic and tasty it's because the chicken that laid the eggs was free to roam in peace and not forcefully locked in a cage.

Organic meat is healthier, it has less saturated fat and more beneficial omega 3 fatty acids. With an animal living a natural life, being fed with grass and not injected with growth chemicals, you can enjoy the taste of organic growth. So apply organic growth to your middle marathon stage and **reap the rewards** of allowing things to develop naturally.

One thing you shouldn't do in life is be hesitant, as there is a difference between letting things naturally develop and being half-hearted with your actions. It is wiser to decide what you want to do and then go ahead and do it without double questioning your actions.

Do not not half step in life, because if you hesitate a jump, that could be the reason you fall.

Don't be half hearted in anything you do and never allow yourself to continuously be hesitant with what you want to do. I often analyse a situation before I commit, but once I have decided it is for me then I am all in.

I passed my driving test when I was 17 years old because I didn't hesitate with my actions.

Being non-hesitant portrays self confidence.

Perseverance

Middle marathon adversities can be conquered by pure perseverance.

Everyone who is successful has had to persevere at some stage and has also continued to persist through many more obstacles even after becoming a success. So by having perseverance in your arsenal, you will have the trait you'll need to beat turmoils on the route to making progress and even beyond becoming a success.

The trees we see all around us persevere through cold winter seasons each and every year and in the process of doing so, the trees grow stronger because the roots of the tree go deeper into the soil during the cold. You can actually gain strength by persevering through difficulty.

The pain we feel when stretching our muscles literally expresses physically that from pain we can make progress.

Persevering through a tough stretching session will result in you becoming more flexible.

Allow this to express to you that if you persevere through difficulty, then you can improve and you will be building up a strong tolerance towards adversity because by pushing through the pain **you will be stronger tomorrow than you are today**.

As I mention in the future chapter called 'The Power of Perspectives', the treadmill perspective expresses how by going through difficulty we gain strengths. So through each middle marathon setback or obstacle, we can learn to gain insight from our troubles and then elevate ourselves and improve our ways. As we all commonly know, perseverance pays!

Someone who has perseverance in their arsenal will always outdo someone who doesn't on the rocky road to success. I hear Bodybuilders always say "No Pain, No Gain" so persevere through the pain and reap its gain. Just as the muscles grow through tension and pressure, we can grow our character through adverse circumstances.

People who refuse to give up, remain persistent, and don't get discouraged easily when their efforts don't get instantly rewarded, will in due time be rewarded for such characteristics. When persistently trying to achieve something, you will be catapulting yourself in the direction of obtaining the life you want. Ensure you uphold these traits even when something doesn't happen as quick as you anticipated.

Imagine a treasure hunter getting discouraged because of a lack of treasure and then he packs up and quits one quest before he finds his most valuable chest.

Now of course I'm not saying persistently do a job that isn't rewarding, but I am stating that persistence will pay off in the long run, so reap what you sow and don't quit too soon because of a lack of instant reward.

The farmer doesn't expect the crops to grow in an instant but the time will come when all the crops have turned into stock in shops.

Never give up due to small hurdles, as you wouldn't stop your journey driving because of a section of speed bumps slowing you down or due to traffic. Don't let minor setbacks stop you from moving forward; slow progress is better than none at all.

Rivers gain their force by continuous flow, so keep moving forward and become a force of nature yourself. Don't be stagnant like a pond and begin to rot in the process. Simply just keep things flowing. **At times you might need a small**

break to refuel your energy but a time-out with the purpose to refuel is a progressive step in itself.
Do not stop moving forward.

Remember:

"Boats sometimes sail with the waves and wind but sometimes need to sail against waves and wind to get to a desired destination. In life sometimes all things around you may seem to be going against you, but keep pushing through the adversities and you'll end up where you desire to be."-Sean Walsh

You have to persevere through failures on the road to becoming a success. *I believe a success is someone who is constantly working on their development regardless of their circumstance or finances.*

It's important that we understand disappointments can lead to greater understanding.

In life we must allow all of our failures and negative happenings to uplift and develop us in one way or another. When we feel disappointed with someone, we need to acknowledge that we now have more understanding of that person's capabilities. Or if we feel disappointed in ourselves because our plans didn't work out as intended, we shouldn't beat ourselves up about it because those who are a success had to fail many times in the process of finding the formula of achieving their aspirations.

Patience

Patience will limit you from making bad decisions in times of turmoil.

The importance of patience shall never be underestimated. Patience is the ability a person has to face troubles, suffering, and delays without getting agitated, angry or upset. Patience is something we humans always want from others, yet we often ain't patient for others as we ought to be...

Remember that being hasty will lead to waste and patience is key when facing adversities. You can't quit, especially when you once wished to be in the position that you are currently in.

For example:

You once wished to be self-employed and to be your own boss. Now you are and it's getting difficult. You can't quit now. Don't complain about overwhelming amounts of customers when you once wished to be overwhelmed with custom. Install patience and you will reap the rewards of not quitting or making errors in haste.

I want you to keep in mind that many of the world's largest and most successful companies had so many reasons and signs to close down business after very unsuccessful initial years of trade; but with patience they are now extremely established and still ever growing, showing no signs of decline.

Remember those types of companies when going through the middle marathon. Let things play out organically, maintain your perseverance and patience, and then with these tactics you will sail smoothly through tough times.

I'm sure ice cream sales decrease in winter months, but the ice cream man's time is coming!

I'm sure jackets sell less when the sun is shining, but autumn and winter are always on the horizon.

So when in the middle marathon stage, keep patient because your time is coming.

Timing is crucial. Don't rush.

Patience is a true virtue, as some of the sweetest tasting fruits, if picked too soon, can taste the most sour.

"As time ripens the fruit from sour to sweetness, patience can ripen you from struggles to triumphs."
-Sean Walsh

Many of our hurts and frustrations are alleviated through patience. Have you ever heard someone say "just sleep on it and see how you feel?"

Well, if you took that advice in life at any time, then you will know that when you awake from a night's sleep, you feel less bothered by whatever it was causing you turbulence.

You can always turn to patience to alleviate the pressure you feel regarding any circumstances you're facing. Don't feel like you need to rush your recovery to be your best version, because if you do rush the process of feeling better and healing then you may end up actually feeling worse.

Everyone literally feels and heals at their own pace, so patiently allow yourself the time you require to reconnect and recover from whatever it is you are going through.

Patience is a true skill. Many individuals consider themselves patient, but when faced with a situation that could use some, this seems to be the last option they'll turn to after trying to force a way first. Being patient can actually take you in a better direction than always trying to force happenings ahead of their gradual development.

Haste is Waste:

Do not be hasty at all. By doing tasks in urgency it's very likely the task will not be done correctly...

Cooking food with haste changes the taste noticeably. Driving your car with urgency increases the risk of an accident massively. The same applies to business, with haste, mistakes get made and can end up ruining your reputation, so to be patient is a counter-attack to hasty errors.

Haste is the inability to wait, so patience will subdue any actions of scurry.

Propel yourself towards a brighter future by developing the traits of those who are successful.

If you rush around and you are always in a hurry, you will in the grand scheme of things actually make less progress, because you will be highly likely to make mistakes and errors while being in a constant rush; even down to the smallest things in life.

I haven't even mentioned that people who are hasty are increasingly stressed. Remember:

With preparation comes peace and with haste comes mistakes.

Don't allow yourself to continuously be hasty; prepare for the future instead of rushing towards it and being erroneous in the process. It's a wise choice to limit future adversities and you could do just that with having a little more patience; resulting in increased peace.

Have you ever heard of the phrase:

"Hold your horses."

So short but yet so sweet. This is a statement I'll always hear in my fathers voice, may he rest in peace.

Do not be too quick to jump or trot towards your progression and be hasty in the process.

HASTE = WASTE

PREPARATION = **PEACE**

Slow down, genuinely, what is the rush?

We must enjoy our lives, as we aren't going to be on this planet forever. We have at maximum not much more than 100 years to live!

Don't rush through your beautiful existence, you are living. Don't be too concerned with where you're going, embrace where you now stand!

Whilst rushing you won't be able to notice the beauty in your surroundings, this is why I say with preparation comes peace. I want you to imagine a situation:

You are in the taxi on the way to the airport to return home, you've left late, and now you're stressed and anxious you're going to miss your flight.

You don't notice the beauty passing by your taxi window in such circumstances.

But

If you prepared yourself and left sooner, then you would've had a peaceful drive and you would've noticed all the beautiful palm trees swaying in the warm wind.

If you are always focussed on the results then you'll always be halfway there instead of enjoying the journey and embracing how far you've come since the beginning. You may be in the position right now that you once prayed for, don't allow haste to stop you from acknowledging the journey of progress.

You should love what you do and do what you love.

I'll say it once more, **haste is wasteful and with preparation comes peace.**

Alleviate yourself of difficulties.

If you won the jackpot of a million bucks, no one could get on your nerves for a while right?

Why? Because of the big win?

So money gain can increase and maintain your happiness?

Well what if you were offered 5 million pounds but you lose your life in a year's time...

Would you accept the proposal?

You, just as I, would reject that offer right?

So that means you value life more than money, but you don't consciously think of this from day to day and that's why you allow tedious things to get in the way of your happiness.

We have now established that we do actually value life more than money, so increase and maintain your happiness because **you are alive.**

If truckloads of money can stop you from getting down, then simply breathing should stop you from getting down because it is far more important than millions of pounds.

Look, life is precious, you shouldn't allow anything external to harm you internally to the point where you aren't happy. I know it is so much easier said than done and we don't always choose how we feel at times, but just pause for a second.

Fill your lungs with oxygen and consciously be grateful that you're breathing.

If you had 100 million and were the king or queen of a kingdom, there would still be nothing more precious than the very oxygen you are now breathing.

If we fully understood the depths of how the ocean, plants, algae and cyanobacteria create oxygen, it would take our breath away, so don't be overwhelmed by the pressures of life. Simply breathe, relax and embrace life itself.

WORN OUT WORKERS

In this section we will discuss how being overworked and becoming worn out can do you more harm than help.

The reality is when you are worn out and fatigued you will be more likely to make mistakes and you could actually be less productive.

This is why I state that **rest is a form of progress,** and although resting is something I find hard to do because I always want to be putting active effort into bettering my situation. The reality is that at intervals, we will be doing ourselves a favour by choosing rest over action because when we become fatigued and worn out we will not be our best version. This is exactly why some of the world's best sports players don't compete in every single game.

I'll ask you a question…

Would you allow a loved one to drive while they are really tired?

No, I wouldn't either because of the increased chance of an accident.

No one consciously chooses to fall asleep at the wheel but it still happens.

Allow this analogy to express to you how tiredness can lead us into errors and accidents, even when we consciously choose not to.

Fatigue is an ingredient that makes us all less productive, so I'll say it again,

resting is a form of progress.

Did you know that it is so common to be exhausted that there is a acronym for it,

'TATT' which means 'tired all the time.'

Whether it's from spending excessive hours working, a baby keeping you awake at night, insomnia or just too many late nights due to lack of a routine; it is almost normal to be 'TATT', but this truly isn't normal at all.

If you feel tired all the time, then you most definitely need to alter the life you live because this will massively impact your standard of life.

Of course, if you are tired and you are always on the move, then you will require an increase in resting time. However, some of my most mentally tired times came when I wasn't being productive at all, so to counter-attack that mental fatigue you may need to actually be more active than seeking more rest.

Do not be quick to declare you're tired either, because you will feel more tired as a result of this, as I previously mentioned with **self diagnosis**.

There is no harm in going to the GP to do a blood test to double check if you have any deficiencies causing the constant fatigue. All of us living in the colder countries lack

Vitamin D due to less sunlight, so experiment to find your most energetic and lively version.

The physical causes of tiredness are actually less common than the psychological causes which are:

Depression: If you have ever felt depressed, then you will understand this more clearly, but for those who haven't, with depression you can literally wake up feeling even more tired than when you went to sleep with a decrease in both mental and physical energy, which then leads to even more sadness and self-induced guilt.

Anxiety: Overwhelmed by feelings of anxiety and pressure can make an individual extremely tired because it could lead to lack of sleep at night due to the anxious thoughts and can have you feeling fatigued due to the constant pressure from external situations, most of which in reality don't exist.

Stress: The pressure of daily life can at some point cause us to feel tired before the day has begun because we are aware of all that we are expected to do. We may not always have the energy to uphold our schedules and this is why I advise everyone to try to find a job they enjoy because it will alleviate a large amount of future mental burdens. Even if the job you enjoy pays less it will be wiser to accept that job instead, as you will be gifted with more mental energy.

One aspect I advise is to make sure you are well fed whilst working. I used to teach kickboxing to under 16's and I never ate from 11am until 7pm daily and then I'd train on an empty stomach and yes I made that job so much more difficult by not fueling myself correctly.

The next time you feel overworked and low in mood, remind yourself why you begun, who you are doing it for and remember how you felt when you weren't doing anything productive with your time.

Many individuals forget how bad it felt when they weren't working. People feel worthless when they can't find employment so I remind myself of this to limit my complaints of working.

"It is better to suffer on the journey of achievement than to suffer by being dormant."-**Sean Atlas Walsh**
People suffer mentally just as much as financially when not working, so limit your complaints of being overworked by remembering at least you're progressing through the adversity.

My nan continues to work daily even into her elderly years and she is always up and wide awake before 6am. She has worked her whole life and uses work as a coping mechanism.

My nan no longer needs to work for financial reasons but it provides her with something to do and when I call her to see how she is, she often jokes with me that,

"I've just been working. It keeps me out of trouble." I can actually hear her voice as I type this; she's been working in London for 50 plus years.

Don't make work more adverse by viewing it solely as a daunting task when your job could actually be providing you with an increase in positive psychological well-being. That includes having a heightened sense of self worth, purpose, stability, better social life and more income so you can then enjoy or treat yourself once the work is done.

My nan saying work keeps her out of trouble is only a joke but in reality many individuals, if they weren't working, would be doing the wrong things; so I understand what she means.

Mother's Day Everyday

Mother's Day should be every single day. Mums sacrifice so much to raise a child that they even sacrifice their own physical health. Did you know one in three women have weakness in their bladders after birth known as 'urinary incontinence.'

To the men reading this: it is important you understand the depths of a mother's role because it is your duty to reassure the women in your family that they're doing a good job. Do not allow a lady in your family to begin to feel like she's achieving nothing when she's raising a child, because the role of a mother is a lot more challenging than our workplace. Many women become mothers and then experience postnatal depression.

The symptoms of postnatal depression consist of lack of energy, to feelings of continuous sadness, so it is our duty as partners, family, and friends of new mothers to reassure them as well as remind them of the great job they're doing. Comprehend this:

We can complain about the hours we are working, but guess what? Being a mother is a 24 hour, 7 days a week job, with constant needs and lack of sleep.

Keep this in mind if your partner seems to get angry abruptly or if your friend who is a new mum begins to act slightly differently.

In life, when an ambitious woman becomes a mother, she sacrifices her career path for at least a number of years. So as a companion of a new mother, just be reassuring to them and praise them for the job they're doing.

Ask them would they rather still be working whilst their child is young and have less of a loving connection in the long run with their children?

I once dated a famous chef's daughter and because both her parents were so career driven, she openly admits that she has more love in her heart for her carer than her own parents. The mothers who did have to continue their jobs to maintain the household shouldn't regret doing so because maintenance is vital.

On the other hand, mothers shouldn't feel less of a success because they have put their careers on pause to perfectly raise their children because it won't last forever. Once your children grow up and you have more free time again, you may actually have an increased work-rate and work harder than ever before. You always hear successful people stating, "Having children is my biggest most meaningful motivation." A new mother will need even more support in the first few months of giving birth. Not many men my age understand the extent of the changes a new mother goes through. Imagine having to be cautious when coughing because you could wet yourself.

A new parent shall never be left to feel like they have lost their own potential now that they have children. The children you raise will be your lifelong best friends and they're half of you and half of your partner. Life is such a blessing but ensure you help the women in your family to not get down and depressed during parenthood.

This section may seem off-topic, but it's important that we acknowledge that our female companions can suffer through the journey of parenthood and just a small amount of reassurance can alleviate a fraction of their stress and sadness.

Yesterday I saw my mum unexpectedly and then me and my sisters took her for some nice food. In our circumstance, we see our mum very few and far between and it was such a good day to see and spend some time with her.

Yesterday was a rare occurrence, so the moments became important memories that I will always treasure. If your parents and grandparents are still alive, call them and plan to meet because time waits for no one and it moves by so quickly. It's important you make memories with each other, don't be shy to be the first person to show love. Many of the older generations were raised in stubborn ways, so break the cycle and reassure all your family that you love them and you are grateful to have them in your life.

PACE YOURSELF

The reality is if you want too much too soon, you will end up ruining gradual development. Individuals who always strive for more but are content with what they have whilst doing so, will be doing themselves good by aiming for more. On the other hand, the individuals who are never happy with what they have, always want more, and fail to pace themselves, will very likely result in them causing more harm than help towards their development.

The pirate's greed can sink his ship. The pirate who strives for his fair share sails smoothly.

Do not force or rush your progress. **Do not allow greed to sabotage your ascendence** and result in problems. Greed comes in many forms. I see some people always wanting more for less work-rate than others. Some go on bargain hunts, whether that be for a new car or a new washing machine. By being greedy with your money you'll end up buying something that is close to breaking and won't last long.

I myself until only recently spent a maximum of three thousand on a car, and guess what…

I needed a new car every 6-12 months!

It is far wiser to invest in things that are longer lasting. Pace yourself into becoming your best version. It's better to organically grow, avoid being greedy, and ascend slowly into better circumstances.

If you went to the gym for the first time and attempted lifting heavy weights that no one can lift on their first day, you will leave the gym feeling deflated and weak. Yet if you pace yourself and begin at your own level, then you will actually start to increase your strength, all by going at your own pace until one day the heavy weights don't feel so heavy.

Pacing yourself is a great way to further your self development because you will be operating at your own levels and being consistent in doing so will result in your levels increasing whilst not feeling as much difficulty as if you were always doing more than you're capable of.

Think of this, when a long distance runner is about to begin a marathon…
Do you see them sprinting? Or do you see them **pace themselves** for the long road ahead?
Do not burn yourself out by being impatient and pace yourself so you don't over-exert energy when you may need it. Preserve it for the potential challenges ahead.
It is always wiser to go at your own pace.
Yes it is good to always push yourself, but if you pace yourself continuously in life (as with the long distance runner) you will actually be making more progress and avoiding accidents and errors so it is wiser to pace oneself.
What do physiotherapists say the majority of the time to those coming back from injury?
"Pace yourself and take it easy."
Why?
Because it is wiser to slowly progress and recover than to be impatient and run the risk of more accidents or injuries.
I'm not a medic or physiotherapist, but I have put to practise this advice to other aspects of life and have come to realise that we can apply such wisdom to many different parts of life and reap the benefits.
Do the maths on this:
Returning to the analogy of the long distance runner; one runner doesn't like to pace himself and as a result he needs a day's rest after each run because he exceeded his limits.
He runs 7 miles on running days, so that is 21 miles per 6 days, amazing!

Then there is the woman who prefers to pace herself throughout the week but runs daily. She opts to run 2 miles less than the man who doesn't pace himself and after doing so she has the capability to run day after day consistently without much fatigue. Now let's do the maths; the man ran 3 times in 6 days, the runs were 7 miles each which is 21 miles, and the woman who paces herself ran 6 out of 6 days and runs 5 miles per day. So who ran more miles in a 6 day span? **The woman who paced herself**. She ran 30 miles in 6 days. Allow this example to show you that you can, in your day-to-day life, make more progression with pacing yourself rather than constantly trying to push against your limits. The woman ran 5 miles a day rather than 7 every other day on this 6 day calculation. Overall she ran 9 more miles than the man.

Pacing yourself is progressive and it enables progression with less adversity.

I believe it is better to pace yourself and do daily actions continuously to further develop oneself rather than enter the **boom and bust cycle**.

The **boom and bust cycle** in business is episodes of expansion and success followed by recession and declination.

Individuals can experience boom and bust cycles in their daily lives as well. This happens when an individual may do too much one day and then feel unable to do anything the following day. This is why it is wise to pace yourself.

As with the famous story of a slow but successful tortoise becoming the unlikely winner of a race, we should learn to increase our daily energy and limit our mistakes. This is all a consequence of simply pacing ourselves instead of being hasty or pushing through too much adversity.

It is absolutely normal to have both good and bad days, as we all do, but when pacing yourself this will result in you not feeling like you have too much to do because you know you are capable of doing what you have been consistently doing. Don't think that just because you're pacing yourself that you can't increase your effort. You can gradually increase your efforts, but maintaining continuous efficiency is more important than pushing your limits to the point of tiredness. After gradually increasing your effort you will reach a positive position of pacing yourself at the level of other's maximum effort. By doing this you will benefit yourself in abundance and you will ensure you are always progressing. **You will continuously be doing daily tasks which will benefit your tomorrow.**

In life, if you pace yourself, then you won't have an overload of work or anxiety to deal with and even on the bad days you still get done what you always set out to do. Plus,on the good days, when you have high energy, you don't exhaust yourself by doing more than you need to. **Pacing yourself will limit your tiredness of tomorrow!**

We also have to remind ourselves that from darkness comes light, and through difficulties comes ease. After anger comes peace, and all times of turmoil ultimately lead us to become better people if we approach them the right way.

The middle marathon struggles will have you appreciating when things start going well.

If everything was perfect all the time, then it wouldn't truly feel perfect, because you wouldn't know the difference.

A person once homeless now appreciates the roof above their head.

A person once poor and hungry now appreciates all food and doesn't waste any.

A person complaining in their car about traffic should try standing at a cold bus stop in the rain.

A rich man, who was so rich, but still felt emotionally empty, realises that life isn't all about money. All hardships enhance our futures if reacted to correctly. Our reactions are more important than what has happened to us because our reactions determine our future and what has happened gets deeper into the past as each day goes by So organically, patiently, or through pure perseverance, move through the middle marathon and incline into a place of more success and happiness.

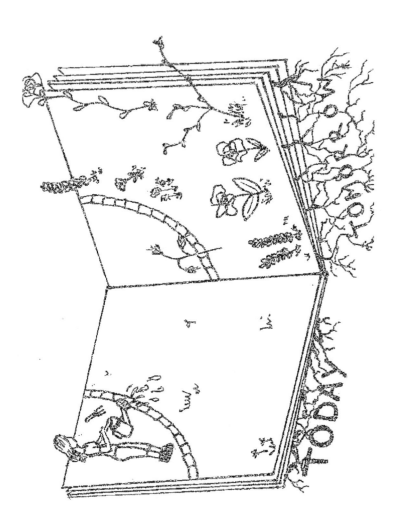

Artwork by Annalise B.

5
TOMORROW BEGINS TODAY

Tomorrow begins today because at maximum, tomorrow is only 24 hours away, but by the time most of us wake it's most likely only 16 hours away. So do today what benefits your tomorrow.

If you live by making your future self proud, then you'll know at times that current temptations and emotions can be outweighed by the bigger picture to aid your daily progress and lofty aspirations.

Yes, of course it wouldn't be an exciting idea to do some study revision when your friends are out partying, but when you find yourself in that exam hall you will be very thankful that you chose to do so. Your good choices yesterday enhanced your today, and your decisions today will enhance tomorrow.

If you do today what aids your tomorrow, you will give yourself the best chance of progress and you'll also conquer some mental adversities because **with preparation comes peace.** Being at your best will enable you to complete tasks with ease.

For example:

Choosing to have an early night's sleep today, instead of staying up late watching TV, will give you the best chance at getting enough rest. This enables you to be recharged and ready for the day and its challenges. Without enough sleep you decline mentally, then the decision the night before was very important to the quality of the next day. It doesn't just have you uplifted in energy, it will also limit or conquer mental and physical adversities.

It is scientifically proven that getting enough sleep lowers the stress hormone called **cortisol**. With lower levels of cortisol you're less stressed, meaning you'll be much happier and all-in-all more focussed.

No more trying to cut corners. Real progress in abundance comes from making the right choices. You will have to ensure you get enough rest. This isn't just about physical rest. Have you ever experienced mental fatigue whilst having physical energy?

I never experienced this until I began writing this book because I was always passionate in regard to physical exercise, so I never felt mentally tired with physical energy before this. I feel like the experience I have had with being mentally tired whilst physically energetic will further my understanding of how both our mental and physical energies both need our attention and fair share of rest.

This experience will enable me to be able to give advice to others on becoming aware of the fact that we needn't just give attention to our physical health, but that mental health needs resting and attention as well.

Maintenance is important and you will need to maintain a good amount of rest because you can cause more damage than assistance when constantly feeling and pushing through tiredness.

Those who are successful are often regarded as lucky, but what people fail to realise is that when an opportunity arises and you are prepared for it, then the circumstances are ready for you to flourish. When always prepared for opportunities, you'll never not be ready for elevation. So stay **prepared,** stay **ready** and **become lucky.** Success doesn't come easy. You can't be successful without making some form of sacrifice.

People often assume success comes to fruition in the case of luck or special circumstances, but many people trail-blazed their own path to success through their own personal sacrifices and by remaining prepared at all times. This takes daily effort, so to be lucky means you have to be prepared at all times. For when that special opportunity arises and by making decisions today that helps your tomorrow, it enhances your chances of success.

For example:

A boxer who stays in shape all year round and maintains being close to his fighting weight gets a call 4 weeks out to replace an injured opponent. Due to staying prepared, the fighter is in a much better position to take on the fight and actually win, so called 'lucky success'.

Apply this to your life and you'll always be ready for whatever arises. By not being prepared for future opportunities it means you are technically battling yourself before you even begin. It's as if Jekyll is holding back Hyde from succeeding. Living by this method, you will have more physical energy and this increases your willingness to do exercise for your wellbeing. Increased energy also helps any physical aspects of work, as you will not feel deflated or lazy towards your daily duties or chores.

You literally become a new person with propelled physical and mental energy. With the increased mental energy, you will be more focused and engaged in all aspects of life. The results of more mental energy are limitless, especially more willingness to learn, which will lead to more career opportunities opening up. You'll absorb so much more information, and I know this through first hand experience because when at school, going through really tough times at home and then living alone since 14, I never had enough sleep the day before to absorb the classes I was in. It affected my physical and mental energy greatly; I was the complete opposite of ready to learn. I was even occasionally falling asleep at the school desk. Maybe it was a lack of sleep or maybe a lack of interest in Macbeth, but I know for a fact that if I lived back then with a mindset of **tomorrow begins today** then I would've absolutely ingested more information. You will reap the rewards of doing today what betters your tomorrow.

As you are improving,

And you are improving,

You'll begin to notice.

You can be a better version tomorrow than you are today, but only by making the right decisions in this very moment. You will need to not care about the opinion of others because this is about you becoming your own best friend and taking actions towards being your own best version.

People will hold their own viewpoint of you regardless, so pay no attention to the opinions of others. For example: a man who was previously an alcoholic but hasn't touched alcohol in 10 years by some will still be judged as a drunk; but do you think their opinions matter?

No. What does matter is that the man doesn't return back to his old ways of living and he will do just that by doing today what will benefit his tomorrow.

Begin at once to not pay attention to the opinions of others. Rather focus on the steps you can take daily to better your beginnings of tomorrow.

The right choices to better your tomorrow consist of personal things to yourself. Ask yourself…

What do you feel you could change to better benefit you and your life?

You can install habits to improve yourself in any aspect of your life. Do not put off improving yourself today until tomorrow because it means you'll be a day behind where you could've been. *Instantaneously change everything you have control over that will benefit the future you.*

What did you do yesterday that affected today badly?

You have to be completely honest with yourself… what do you continuously do that you deep down know isn't good for you? What is it that you do daily or even weekly that isn't truly good for you or affects the following day negatively?

It's good to install new habits, but it's even more important to remove the bad habits you have. Begin today to better your tomorrow.

What did you do yesterday that impacted today positively?

As I mentioned in Passion Pursuit, being passionate about something can provide you with so much more positivity. I want you to become more conscious of the actions which have a positive effect on the tales of tomorrow. When you become aware of what truly enhances your life the following day, as your own mental pilot, you can decide to do daily actions which will affect you in positive ways.

Do you really utilise your free time?

Many individuals claim they have no free time to follow their passions or to spend on themselves, but these same people will spend an hour or two a day on social media.

Make sure you utilise the free time you do have; we do have enough time daily to do the most important things but it all comes down to your own decision making.

Do you leave everything until the last minute?

Leaving tasks until the last moment can get very stressful, so conquer that stress by not leaving them until the last moment.

A page of the day's to-do list will increase your productivity because you will complete all you intended to and you won't leave what can be done today to get in the way of tomorrow's task. As you tick off each task you complete, you will feel positively productive and you will be avoiding an overwhelming tomorrow filled with tasks from the day before. I personally get more done by simply writing down what I need to do on a daily basis, as I won't forget all the smaller tasks that need doing. It is better to complete tasks one by one entirely and correctly than multitask and do things improperly. Having your to-do list in priority order is also crucial, as you don't put off critical tasks due to lack of enthusiasm and enjoyment.

Do you get stressed about arriving on time to work?

If so, why not leave 5 or 10 minutes earlier to conquer that stress…

Remember with preparation comes peace so, limit pressure and stress by using this method. Leaving a little earlier can cancel out anxiety regarding arriving on time.

Whatever you feel you can alter to improve your days, then absolutely *do it*.

These small changes are personal to your circumstance, so put this chapter to practise and enjoy the results of progression and days of less stress.

Do you feel like pressure pushes you to increase your efforts and performance?

If so, then continually put pressure on yourself today and tomorrow to ensure you consistently perform at a high level. Pressure isn't such a bad thing to feel, as it will push you to be productive everyday. It's impossible for pressure to be a negative experience if it is exactly what is resulting in your best performance.

DISCIPLINE

It is very important towards your development that you install and maintain levels of discipline on a daily basis.

Discipline helps us to create positive habits and these habits will then become a part of our routines and the heights of success and self Improvement we reach will massively rely on how we live out our daily lives. The person we become will reflect our routines.

Be sure to consciously choose to be disciplined, although at intervals we will give into different forms of temptation, it is wise to continually be conscious about discipline because you will be planting positive seeds into your subconscious and eventually positive decisions will become automatic ways of living.

Individuals who are disciplined daily have an increased chance of achieving their aspirations and maintaining consistency in their characters. Discipline is when you complete what needs to be done and restrain from indulging in the aspects of life you should be avoiding.

People who are disciplined will stay on track to achieve success because they will remain focussed on the goals they have set and being disciplined will assist them into better decision-making.

You will develop much more self control when trying to be disciplined. As I said, at times we may make a mistake, but **we shouldn't allow one ill-disciplined day to create an ill-disciplined week.**

If you do have a bad day, return to being back to your disciplined version the very next day. Tomorrow begins today, so don't allow one mistake to mess up your week.

It is progressive in itself that you're even conscious of discipline because you will develop more self awareness and focus. Ask yourself:

Would you employ an individual who is disciplined and focussed or an impulsive and unaware person? Attempting to increase your discipline is a very positive and meaningful aspect of life to give your energy to. You will develop in multiple ways when doing so and work will become easier as you will be keeping yourself in the best position to complete tasks.

Real genuine discipline is the amount of control you have over yourself, especially in very tempting or out of your comfort zone situations. Many people claim they're disciplined but haven't faced such tempting or adverse circumstances in life. It is wise to try to build up your discipline every single day, for who knows what the future holds.

The most beautiful part about discipline is that the level of how disciplined we are is entirely up to ourselves. It is quite literally all in our own power because no one but ourselves can increase or decrease our discipline.

If you're around many things tempting you to break your discipline, this is the opportunity to actually strengthen it. As I said, only you can increase or decrease your discipline and when presented with temptations to give in, keep in mind that this is your chance to increase the strength of your resilience.

Tomorrow begins today, so perpetually increase your strength in discipline because this will lead you to a life of progression and healthier living.

One aspect I am disciplined with is the use of my time. **I believe we have so much opportunity to utilise our time throughout the day,** but we throw hours away to so many pointless things such as spending hours on social media or hours on the phone gossiping. **We have to begin to be disciplined with the utilisation of our time** and make efficient use of any spare time we get.

View this time-based discipline as the opposite of multitasking, as it will enable you to complete and focus entirely on one thing at a time with no interruptions. You will improve mentally, physically and spiritually by acknowledging and living in a way that your time is extremely valuable, which it is.

Living life in such a way will make your aspirations that slightest bit easier to obtain because **tomorrow begins today. Therefore we will need to stop wasting time immediately.**

Ask yourself:

How many hours have you spent this month on social media?

How many hours have you spent watching box sets on Netflix?

There is this concept that those who are successful are just lucky, but being prepared, disciplined, and ready for opportunities is not being lucky at all.

Practise the concept of this chapter by being disciplined daily because those who have such characteristics overlook instant satisfaction and rewards for greater success in the future. So live by discipline today and it will benefit your tomorrow. Living like this will provide you with many of the traits successful individuals possess such as:

Installing and maintaining focus on the goals you set and sticking to the plans you've made.

Maintaining positive thoughts and behaviours. Plus, you will be avoiding laziness and procrastination. There is a belief that a disciplined life is nothing but boring and overly sensible, but there is nothing boring about increasingly becoming your best version and strengthening yourself daily through discipline.

Individuals who are disciplined are often more positive, goal driven and sensible people. Being disciplined results in increased self esteem, self control, happiness and positive pride in oneself.

One thing we all know is that life will present us with hardships and challenges at some stage, but by being self disciplined you will be putting yourself in a good position to cope and deal with anything that arises.

Discipline will assist you in achieving what you set out to do and ill-discipline will do the opposite. Stick to the plans you've made and you will be well on your way to becoming a better version.

Self Accountability

You will have to hold yourself accountable starting from today.

You can no longer put the blame on external causes or other people for any aspect of your life that isn't how you'd like it to be. Instead of being quick to point your finger at many different causes of a situation, rather use all of your energy to aim, then fulfil the changes you want to see or to be done in your lifestyle.

The moment you hold yourself accountable is the very moment you can truly make improvements in your own ways, because when a mistake is made, you will reflect on how to avoid it happening in the future and improve on your error, instead of pushing the blame onto others or many different causes. You will now use a mistake that you've made to assist you in improving.

Self development becomes a lot easier when you hold yourself accountable. The aspects through which you can personally better yourself will be easier to notice as you will become more self aware. You will also be able to accept when something goes wrong. Others limit their levels of development in life by not holding themselves accountable and not accepting where and when they went wrong; don't limit your ascendancy to your best version by being stubborn in error.

Resisting admittance of an error only makes it more difficult to acknowledge the methods one can use to better their ways. Holding yourself accountable will assist you in being more motivated, as well as you being aware that it is up to you to make things happen, ultimately **your actions will determine where you will end up in life.**

You will also be increasing your confidence, not only because you are aware of your own capabilities, but because you will have the humility to admit when you need assistance and in which aspects of life you need to work on to get better at. **Many people deflate their confidence by not admitting their capabilities** and committing to something they aren't entirely prepared to take on. With self accountability you will expand your capabilities because when you need help or you're struggling, you will be able to ask for assistance and then you will be able to reflect on what you can do to progress instead of blaming others.

You will gain the growth mindset when being self accountable because **you will not allow stubbornness to limit the ways in which you can grow and develop further.**

You won't self diagnose limitations because you will always be open to learning new ways of doing things and learning different skills to expand your capabilities.

I will mention later in 'Consciousness' that it is always wise to experience more and learn new things because our consciousness creates our reality. So by having self accountability you will be open to discovering more, and as a result, you will be expanding your capabilities in reality.

Progression is a consequence of character, so if you remain consistent in character today, then you will make progress daily. When I state that tomorrow begins today it is because what we do today will always impact our tomorrow and this is an everlasting cycle. There is no escaping it, so be wise and do daily actions which will benefit the following day. **Be disciplined with consistency in your character.** Lastly, those who hold themselves accountable do not blame external causes for the aspects of life which they have control over or the aspects they have the power to improve. These individuals work on improving things today to better and benefit their tomorrow, so always hold yourself accountable because you will guarantee self improvement.

"A person who holds themselves responsible for errors made will always find it easier to improve upon their ways."

-Sean Atlas Walsh

I want to express a situation in which you should hold yourself more accountable.

Imagine one day a person woke up and felt down and upset so they cancelled their plans and remained at home all day. Then, they began to ponder on their feelings and as a result ended up overthinking. Now this is why I state that **thinking and not taking action to feel better will increase your anxieties.**

If that person was a loved one would you advise them to stay home and remain in constant overthinking which will only increase their adversities?

Or would you advise them to use that energy to take action towards feeling better?

If they were to take immediate action, I can guarantee, although initially difficult to do so, that the individual will experience less anxious thoughts by simply going on a walk or to meet a friend than if they remained at home pondering on their problems.

Of course it is easier said than done. People who experience anxiety wouldn't want to leave the house because initially that will increase their anxieties but what is better…

To remain at home and experience negative overthinking without the mood changing, or to have the courage to walk towards changing the ways that you're feeling? More often than not the anxious thoughts aren't even reality. For those who feel like everyone is constantly watching them, although it may feel like absolute reality to that individual, the truth is everyone isn't watching you and you shouldn't allow such thoughts to limit the life you live. ***Begin today to walk with courage over cowardice and with faith over fear.***

If you take action to avoid overthinking an outcome, you will not only halt stressing over possibilities, but you will also be creating one when taking positive action. You'll be your best mental pilot.

You will have to take self accountability when it comes to negatively affecting your mental health. I'll give an example: Individuals who experience anxious thoughts and feel judged by others, which then causes them stress, is it wise for those individuals to be on social media exposing their life on an online platform?

It isn't very wise is it? People fail to acknowledge that their actions play the most crucial part in the ways they are feeling and I know people who do this continuously in oblivion and go around and around causing themselves adversity.

I never feel anxious when posting a part of my training videos or some content of my book. What does cause me anxiety is that I take pride in the way I present myself, so when I was continually using Snapchat for so many years, for one it consumed many hours of my life and secondly, it also led me to double check everything I was posting so that I made certain I was presenting myself well. If you're a very anxious person I will advise you to remove social media or post substantially less because with a private life comes a peaceful life.

I recently deleted Snapchat after years upon years of usage because I knew if I did follow through with deleting the app that the following day I would've gained at least an extra hour to be positively productive on a more important aspect of life. **Remove from your life today what will limit or be of detriment to your tomorrow.**

It initially felt weird because I was using Snapchat for years but **it only took a week to get used to not using it.** The very next morning I was at the gym at 6am and I was so used to posting anytime I was at the gym that it was a genuine challenge to not return to being on the app. However, 4 weeks later, I could wholeheartedly say it was one of the best decisions I could've made, as it provided me with at least an extra hour daily to work towards actually achieving something and chasing my aspirations. Not to mention I have increasingly more intense training sessions now that I ain't interrupted by picture-posting.

We must take self accountability on the time we waste or fail to utilise because no one can force us to be productive in the free time we have; so only we are the ones accountable for our time wasted.

Do not blame others for the limitations you allow yourself to remain in.

Temptations

Limit or remove temptations which affect your following day. Firstly, I want to state that no one finds it easy to always reject temptation, so don't be hard on yourself if you do occasionally give in. We are only human and we should also enjoy things that life has to offer, but deterring these temptations in reality can be the difference between success and failure. When there is a group of talented people, more often than not the person who is willing to sacrifice the most will be the front-runner, even if their skill set is lacking. They make up for the lack of skill by better decisions today to enhance their tomorrow. In a group of teenage football prospects, the difference between the life changing football contract and losing out on their childhood dreams could come down to small margins of sacrifice or resistance. The teenager who resisted the temptation of late night video games with friends online in order to get extra sleep before training in the morning, will be the player getting signed; all due to correct decisions today. Small sacrifices accumulate to massive changes. No small change made to improve is irrelevant, as it all adds up to the final equation.

The same applies to students of all ages. Resisting small temptations in order to study a little while longer will enhance your grades on exam papers.

Elevation is always more important than temptation.

Another example I can express is that making choices for the future not only saves you from mental adversity, but also maintains positive momentum. Sometimes when I'm exercising at the gym daily to gain strength and mental stability I get interrupted by being tempted, and then choosing to go out for drinks at a bar. But by not resisting that temptation, I then lost my training momentum, as the next day I was too hungover to train.

Now, although I do enjoy a whisky on ice or a pint of Guinness, I know for the sake of my progress and mental stability, it is not wise of me to indulge in drinking these often. If I reject the invite to go out to the bar, my night will definitely be less eventful and less entertaining, but who will be the one awake early in the morning ready for training and ready for the day and its challenges? Me or the ones out partying? Let the answer show you that sacrificing a night of enjoyment is better for you/me because the party-goers are hungover and sleeping whilst you're progressing and being healthy.

Another method you need to use when facing temptation is to eliminate the things that are tempting you. If you're a person with a sweet tooth, don't keep sweets in your house. If you're dieting and want to stop ordering takeaways, then delete the food delivery apps off your phone. Apply this to anything personal to yourself...

If you want to stop vaping, it isn't wise to keep a vape pen nearby. Make the things you want to stop doing difficult to do, and then it will make it easier to stop.

Even down to a good night's sleep; remove entertainment from your bedroom, as it's always more difficult to sleep when you're one click away from your favourite show.

All things tempting you that deprive you in any way need to be removed from your life. Make sure you do so, as even bad things limited to a place and time lose their bad effects... and even good things in abundance can have bad effects... so this is about removing daily temptations that are affecting your next hour or day.

You can also ask friends to not invite you out at times when you need to stay focussed. It's always wiser to avoid even being tempted than having to feel the urge and then fight against it.

By not practising **tomorrow begins today** you run the risk of procrastination and delaying tasks. This is the complete opposite trait of those who are successful. Inherit the characteristics of successful people.

I'm a big believer that the way you do all the small tasks will have a domino effect on all the more prominent tasks. I once watched a video on YouTube of a person saying that making our beds in the morning is the most important part of our days and I fully agree because if you don't complete those smaller tasks, then you're starting the day off on the wrong foot.

If your first step was in the wrong direction, you will not end up at your desired destination. If a car takes the wrong turn at the beginning of a journey it will be driving in the wrong direction until corrected, so make sure you do all things correctly and create positive momentum.

If you do all things correctly with pride then you will do nothing wrong, and keep in mind with preparation comes peace.

Do not procrastinate, do not keep saying that you will begin tomorrow, because that is just politely rejecting yourself from elevation. **Tomorrow begins today,**
If you keep putting things off until the next day then you are being your own worst enemy. The only difference between starting right now and starting next week Monday is that you will be days behind where you could have been.

Do today what helps your tomorrow.
Your future self will be grateful.

HEALTH

Now, the most important part of our human lives is preserving our health.

I often ask why people take for granted the greatest richness of all, health.

People don't think of their health unless they become ill. To me that's crazy. I want to express something, we always think about earning more money even when we haven't lost any finances, so why do we only seek more health when it's declining?

Riddle me that?

Do not delay preserving your health because without it, all things material will have no meaning. You think when you're breathing your last breath that you're going to be thinking about your wallet?

Ask those in hospitals in critical condition, do they wish they earned more or lived more?

I think it's quite obvious what the answer will be, so don't wait to regret, rather live a life of beautiful memories you'll never forget.

Why do cigarette smokers only give up smoking after serious health issues?

To me that's like waiting to go through a car crash to then start wearing a seatbelt after surviving the crash...

Please for the sake of not just yourself but your loved ones, start **today** to preserve the greatest richness of all, health.

Tomorrow begins today when it comes to making changes to improve your health because remember every single day people pass away and for some of those people, if they acted sooner on enhancing their health, they could still be with us. Rest in peace to all before us, but please make sure your health is your immediate priority, without it nothing has meaning. Life ends.

Do not wait for a health scare as motivation to be healthier. I wish I was a bit older so I could've tried to prevent my father's early death. It was because he was oblivious to the effects of the substances he was taking. Everything happens for a reason.

Remember:

Those healthy are the most wealthy.

No money can bring back the dead, only healthy decisions today can help extend your lifespan.

Preserving your health results in more years around your friends, family and children.

Life is a blessing we need to enjoy and attempt to extend.

There is a universal law called the law of forced efficiency which states:

There is never enough time to do everything but there is always, always, enough time to do the most important things and preserving health is of utmost significance.

Lastly:

"Your actions yesterday impacted today, as your actions today will impact your tomorrow."

Every small action taken is significant towards the final outcome. If you got one digit wrong on a phone number you will end up calling the wrong person. Allow this analogy to express to you that every single action towards leading you in the right direction is important.

Do not spend another day awaiting a perfect scenario to begin, rather start today so that tomorrow you're already one day in!

I see many people putting off their new beginnings and never taking action. Tomorrow begins today so do today what will influence tomorrow positively.

How does concrete, cement, wood, metal, bricks, glass and sand build a home?

With daily effort of building and putting the parts in place. So do not expect a perfect day to begin because it is unlikely to happen, but do begin to slowly put things into position.

If you are able to actively do good for yourself, by yourself, then you quite literally will never not improve on your ways and you will become a better person day by day. Many people do healthy things conditionally. What I mean by this is, for an individual to be comfortable going to the gym to improve their fitness and health, they will need their training partner with them. Do actions to elevate yourself always. Even if you're alone; you shouldn't need people cheering you on to want to do the actions required to assist you in becoming a better version.

Thoughts become things. The new hairstyle you now have was once just a thought within the head that the new hairstyle is now on.

Everything external comes from within so begin today to become your most internally positive version. Then do so again tomorrow, because the only thing that separates our thoughts from actual happenings is time.

Consciously choose to always counter-attack negative thinking and replace negative thoughts with positivity.

Artwork by Isabella P.

6
PAST NOT PRESENT

Well, in this chapter I want to make you aware that it's very good to learn from past experiences and historic occurrences, but you can't let past encounters affect your future because with burdens and limitations from past experiences it will be very hard to become a new person and enjoy living in the present moment.

We can all learn from our past, but we can't let what we've gone through destroy the mystery of our futures.

We will need to let go of the troubles we've faced in the past to embrace the present moment.

The moment we are living in right now is the most important and we should embrace it entirely. It is called the present because it's truly a gift to be alive in this very moment. Life is a blessing we need to enjoy daily, so don't let the past defeat today's happiness and happenings.

Instead of wasting energy dwelling on past times, use your energy on making the present moment a moment to savour. Although the past will play a huge role in what we are conscious of and how we perceive the world, we shouldn't become a prisoner of our past because then you will be limiting the present day from its potential positive occurrences that you have not experienced. We shouldn't allow the past to cancel our faith in more positive things happening and we shouldn't allow experiences with the wrong people to ruin our potential of meeting genuinely good people. **Strangers aren't always strange, so be willing to meet new people with an open mind.** Many people have placed their trust in the wrong hands and now live the rest of their days not trusting anyone. I see many people always saying 'trust no one' and to be very honest I think the people who say this the most cannot even trust themselves.

If someone in the past has broken your trust, don't let that continually affect your trust in others because if you know that trust is safe when it is placed with you, then you know wholeheartedly that it is possible to be placed with someone else in confidence. However, when you make new friends don't be so quick to trust them with everything, let the friendship develop, as some people will only be around you for their own interest and benefits. To avoid making the mistake of misplacing your trust, don't open up 100 percent to everyone because it will lead you to lack trust in those who are actually trustworthy.

I live by giving 100% respect and common trust when I first meet someone, which is the best first step to take at the beginning of a new friendship and it has worked well for me because I don't let bad experiences with others impact the start of a present friendship. This way, it is now in the new friend's hands to maintain that trust and respect, which could lead to a stronger social network and not blocking new friendships or they simply don't fit in with you and you remove them from your social group. People are fully aware of their actions, so don't be ignorant and overlook those who have broken your trust. Still, most definitely don't allow past experiences with the untrustworthy affect you from trusting those who are deserving, as this will leave you with a limited possibility of new good relationships. If you use my first steps when initially meeting someone you will end up with a network of good people and more importantly, with those who have similar morals to yourself.

I could've easily allowed the pests of the past to poison my chances of meeting new people, especially coming from a place likened to 'crabs in a bucket', but I never let that impact the potential of new relationships.

Remember:

Those from the past are in the past for a reason.

Hence, now in the present moment, I have multiple 13 year plus friendships, all of which will be like uncles and aunties to my future children and a good business network of those who can rely on me and whom I can rely on.

It is wiser to always be open minded with new people and don't let those from the past poison your present chances of making new relationships. Always start off on the correct foot by being 100% initially. If we allow our past to be of detriment to us we will find it hard to progress into a brighter future.

LOSS OF A LOVED ONE

Past not present also applies to when you've lost a loved one. Although the pain is ever-existing and trust me I know empirically, I lost my best friend who was my father at such a young age and 15 years later I still miss him and feel the loss. Yet his death was in the past and the absolute fact is that those who loved us, who have sadly passed away, would tell us to cheer up and embrace life instead of mourning their loss.

I believe those who have passed away would tell us something along the lines of:

"Live and enjoy every moment, don't waste a single second mourning my loss because life is so precious and needs to be lived in happiness as much as possible."

I only say this because knowing my dads character, if he were to witness the amount of sadness I endured after his loss, he would literally give me a clip around the ear and tell me to not shed anymore tears. Also, when my time to leave Earth comes, I would personally want my loved ones to be celebrating the life and memories we had together and not letting the loss harm their present moments now or in the future.

When we lose a loved one it hurts our soul deeply and it feels like the void will never be filled. Maybe it never will, but we must appreciate the time we did get to spend with those that are gone instead of being sad in the present. We should honour those in the beyond's wishes for us to live life beautifully while we're still here and we can do that by being present in the present.

It's good to relive the past when in reflection to try to improve ourselves or to release pent up emotions, but it has to be limited because we can't go on living our life's mourning forever. Otherwise the dark days will never change. If you keep looking back to what went wrong or against you in the past then your eyes won't recognise the potential positive paths that may open up in front of you.

Everything in life happens for a reason and with every loss there is a lesson. We need to learn from the past and then use those lessons to enhance our presence in the present. Could you imagine a prisoner coming home and finally being free and then all he's ever thinking about and focussed on was when he was in the cell locked up?

How will he see a brighter future if he is focussed solely on the dark past?

How can you notice the beauty of the stars without looking up to the sky? Don't keep your head down due to past suffering; hold your head up high and embrace where you are currently, for you will be able to notice more beauty and positivity in the present by not being focussed on past difficulties. **Looking back on bad times and enabling them to ruin your current feelings and emotions is like complaining about the clouds and heavy rainfall of yesterday and missing out on the clear skies and sunshine of today.**

We have to learn to enjoy the current moment because without it our existence is over. It's impossible to go from the past to the future without the current moment, so remind yourself that **the present moment is the most important**. Energy flows where your focus goes, so let's keep a positive outlook on life and live in the present moment always. Only look back in moments of reflection that are limited to a time and location for self improvement. Don't let the past pollute your future by ruining your present. Be wise.

Time

What do we have between life and death? Time and experiences.

No one is getting younger and we can't turn back the hands of time.

We need to spend our time much more wisely than we spend our finances and this is why I always advise people to travel as much as they can because money comes and goes but time can't be returned. Every single second of our time needs to be as meaningful as possible and we need to make sure we don't waste time pondering on past difficulties. Allowing the past to affect your present is like paying again for a parking fine that you have already paid. Do not double-burden yourself with something you've already paid for and gone through because you won't be spending time wisely and such actions will result in regrets in the future. If you are constantly plagued by what you have been through, then don't feel ashamed to seek help from a counsellor to help you to understand and then overcome the past experiences you have been through. Otherwise you will be less focussed on the good aspects of your life that are right in front of you.

Do not let one negative occurrence cause you continuous suffering, as that will limit the positivity you will feel in the present. It is much wiser to feel then heal and leave the pains of the past in the past, or you will absolutely steal the present of its potential happiness.

As time moves by the past will soon reflect the decisions we make in this very moment and this is why I say,

"Our reaction to happenings is more important than what has actually happened, because our reactions determine our futures and what we have experienced gets deeper into the past as each day goes by."

Right **now** is life. We can't go back to the past so don't let the past badly impact your current day or else when the future comes you will regret the amount of time you spent focusing on the past and not embracing the present.

Invest positively into every single day, as this will conquer many mental pressures and not just from avoiding looking back but also by not putting excessive pressure on where you think you ought to be in the future.

Don't completely be a product of your past because you can decide today to be whatever you want to be. Of course, our past plays a huge role in the development of who we become and the perspectives we have, but we must acknowledge that with active effort we can become whatever we want in the present, regardless of what we have endured in the past. Even with this book I have written, I don't know

another person from my area that is an author. So **you will become a product of your actions more-so than a product of your environment with the determination for change.** Do not limit yourself from fulfilling your potential by condemning your present and future due to past negative experiences because:
"At times a potential crash or bad situation is exactly what we need to learn and change direction."-Sean Atlas Walsh

Forgiveness

It is easier to hold a grudge against someone for something they have done wrong than it is to truly forgive them and move on. Remember I said that what is the easiest for us to do is more often not good for us and this applies to forgiveness as well because it isn't easy to forgive, but it is much wiser for us to do so than to hold onto grudges, anger, and resentment towards someone or a situation.

If you do not forgive those who have done you wrong in the past, then you will be allowing the past to pollute your present because you will feel ongoing negativity from previous experiences such as anger, sadness, resentment and bitterness. So, by forgiving others, you are in fact alleviating yourself from negativity.

Some individuals find it more difficult to forgive than others, but by acknowledging that forgiveness will be helping yourself and avoiding annoyances, it will assist you in becoming more forgiving. Not to mention that forgiveness is a crucial part of multiple religions.

It sounds crazy that many of us allow past happenings to continually affect our present and future moments, but this is exactly what those who fail to forgive are doing.

If you increase your willingness to forgive, you will not only cancel negative thoughts and feelings, but you will also have improved energy and peace of mind. People who don't forgive can become so invested in the past that they will be unable to enjoy their lives in their current situation. These individuals will lose out on new positive aspects of life and relationships by not letting go and moving past previous experiences. **Be forgiving and never block out your present blessings by remaining bitter due to problems you have endured once already.** You must acknowledge that when you are forgiving others for their mistakes you are doing yourself a favour and preventing yourself from negative thoughts, feelings, and emotions. So if you don't want to forgive someone for something they've done, forgive them for yourself to avoid these bad emotions. This isn't about allowing people to do wrong and not be held accountable or to get away with wrongdoing, because **you can forgive and not forget,** but you will prevent the past from igniting anger, hate and resentment in your present moment.

Another way to help assist us in becoming more forgiving is to attempt to understand why and how someone has done wrong or made mistakes. This can make it easier for us to genuinely forgive someone after understanding their perspectives and explanation.

You can reflect back on times when you were the person asking for forgiveness and were forgiven, as this will help you to feel empathy towards the person who wants you to pardon their mistakes. You need to forgive those who don't even seek your remission as well, because as mentioned, it is to prevent yourself from feeling negative burdens.

After understanding the circumstances in which the mistakes were made, it could enable you to be more willing to overcome the mishaps.

I always say, "It is very difficult to fall out with your friends from the church or mosque." This is because that friendship was formed and maintained in a sanctuary and not in adverse circumstances. Many people make friends with others just to use them and don't start the friendship with pure intentions and this is why I think many fallouts happen. Be well aware that you can't always instantly forgive someone, even if you really want to, because more often than not, forgiveness is a process that is unlikely to be instant.

As established, you will be looking out for yourself when forgiving others, so even if it is a process to pardon someone of their wrongdoing, then do so because you will cancel or limit the amount of negative emotions you'll feel in the present from the past. Forgive but don't entirely forget. A person who is forgiving is stronger in strength than the individual who holds onto grudges for years.

If you absolve someone of their wrongs today, you will be alleviating tomorrow of anger, resentment, sadness, bitterness and pain.

The present moment is the most important: take action at once to embrace the now and look forward to the future instead of feeling down over the past you've experienced.

"Forgiveness is an antidote to negative emotions." - Sean Atlas Walsh

Forgive others not because they're always deserving, but because you don't deserve to hold onto the negative emotions that come as a part of holding onto the negativity you feel when someone has done you wrong. **Forgiveness is an act of self love.**

Do not waste energy on being vindictive when you can utilise your energy for something much more positive.

The best form of revenge to someone who is against you is increased self improvement instead of enabling the wrongs of others to limit your positivity and progress.

We must forgive sooner rather than later because we will be avoiding issues from escalating and preventing ourselves from being plagued with negative emotions.

Do Not Judge

Do not judge others solely by their past because people are constantly changing, whether they change for better or for worse. It is always wiser to analyse the characteristics of a person currently and not base it on who they have been in the past.

Someone who was of good character previously could now be entirely different and vice versa, so **do not judge people solely by their past**. Instead, get to know their current version in the present moment because as I mentioned in MENTAL PILOT, the decisions people make daily will change how they feel and who they will become.

I will give you an example of why you shouldn't judge someone on their past.

There was a man from the same council estate in London as my family who was severely bullied in school and even into his late teens. He was sent on errands and was constantly made fun of until one day he couldn't take the abuse anymore. Since then he has gone on to become feared within the community for his willingness to be violent instantly. If you judge this person only by their past, you will be putting yourself in harm's way.

Another example is:

Take an individual who had a drug addiction and was untrustworthy due to their needs, who is now completely clean and hasn't touched drugs in years, does that mean they can never become trustworthy because of their past difficulties?

The brain isn't concrete at all, the brain is in fact ever-growing and constantly changing.

This is exactly how when an individual gets put through practice or therapy they can make conscious progress. Just as you can progress by doing the right things, this is exactly how you can transgress by doing the wrong actions. So limit the judgement of others by viewing their past and **don't judge people for the parts of your life you wouldn't like to be judged on.**

If you criticise someone today for the way they look or an action they've done, this will result in you feeling anxious and judged the next time you are in a similar situation as the person you were judging. Do not increase your future anxieties by being judgemental yourself.

Do not judge anything by appearance for better or for worse, because you will more than likely end up with an item or circumstance that appears good but truly isn't.

Think about it, would you rather an average looking car with a perfect running engine or a supercar with loads of problems but looks amazing?

In life we shouldn't initially judge by image because as with the supercar, it will look so pleasing to the eye but there is always more beneath the bonnet than what the eyes can see. I personally know people who are wealthy but dress so casually and you would never predict they're in the position they're in and I know individuals who look rich and established on Instagram, but in person are in completely different circumstances than what they're advertising. So don't judge only by what meets the eye. This applies to all potential forms of relationships and business.

Those who judge solely by image are more likely to end up with short-lasting relationships and make more mistakes in business.

We shouldn't judge others for the mistakes they have made either. How can you judge an individual's way of dealing with something that you have never been through? No one can completely confirm how they will react to situations until faced with the scenario. Many people claim they're very resilient, determined, and all the other positive characteristics beneath the sun, but when faced with circumstances that challenge them, they fall short. Keep this in mind next time you begin to feel judgemental of others, because you may think you will be able to deal with issues with ease or overcome difficulties easily, but do not judge others even if someone else is less than you in one aspect. I can guarantee they will be better than you at something else in life.

We all have our own strengths and weaknesses. Do not judge because energy comes in full circles. If you judge others you will have increased anxiety at other times because you will feel judged.

It is a natural instinct to have an impulsive judgement of a person or animal but that is deep-rooted from the days when our purpose was solely for survival. What I'm stating is, do not consciously judge anyone excessively.

Don't increase your own anxieties by judging others.

I call this concept **conscious karma**. This is when you begin to imagine and envision the things you've done wrong to others, being done to you.

This is exactly how those individuals who cheat on their partners become the most paranoid or those who have been violent begin to imagine violence being done to them. All because they can envision the wrong they have done being done to them in return, so the same applies to all aspects of life. Treat people how you would like to be treated. We all don't like to be negatively judged by others, but at the same time, we seek constant approval. This is simply impossible. Even religious prophets who lived a selfless and godly life still had multiple enemies and people who hated them. Just as you may not like everyone, not everyone will like you either, but don't criticise others because you will imagine others criticising you.

Now

It's important you embrace the very moment you're living in because in 10 years time you're going to wish you could turn back the clock to be where you are currently. The same way you currently wish you could return to a time or experience in the past is exactly how in the future you're going to wish to return to where you now are. So take a second to inhale the oxygen that surrounds you and wholeheartedly embrace the NOW!

It is all about embracing the present moment because the present will soon be the past. The only way to make the past brighter is to make the current moment a positive moment to remember.

We need to always try our utmost best in the present, for when the future arrives, we can look back at the past and never regret anything as long as we always tried to be our best.

Obviously, energy fluctuates at times and that is completely normal. Do not beat yourself up when feeling down or drained, rather give the present your best even on tired days. Even if your best on those days isn't much at all, it is better than allowing tiredness to make you feel like giving up and quitting.

We don't need to go anywhere fast. Just enjoy where you are, right now, and always do so because then the past will become memories of enjoyment and it will be a pleasure to think about. Plus, the future will always maintain its brightness.

Many individuals cause themselves suffering by always looking back on mistakes or looking too far ahead and feeling less in the now, simply because they aren't appreciating where they now stand. Constantly chasing bigger dreams is a positive way to keep you motivated, but not if thinking of the future makes you never appreciate where you are at in the present moment.

You should only look back in times of reflection or to admire how far you have come!

You should attempt to always make the right decisions in the present to better your beginnings of tomorrow, but always appreciate where you now stand, as the future can only be changed for the better with correct choices in this present moment. Do not ponder on the past or future, but definitely take positive steps in the now towards a brighter path. The past we can't change, but we do have the capability to enhance our futures.

Individuals associate stress as a backlash from negative things, but in reality stress can develop from anything that puts high demands and pressure upon a person or anything that forces them to adjust. This includes positive events as well. For example: getting married, finding and then purchasing the perfect home, completing coursework, responsibility to support family or to perform in front of the public; all of these positive aspects of life can cause excessive stress and anxiety as well.

This is why it's important we embrace only the present moment, because looking back on bad experiences will cause you stress and looking forward to future occurrences can result in you feeling anxious and will be of detriment to your current happiness.

The personal perception of the individual will determine what causes them the most stress. For example, one person may have confidence performing in front of a crowd and can do so easily, but another person will dread the idea of even performing on stage in front of just friends and family.

It's important you do new things in the now to assist you in improving your life. If you haven't been a person of nature in the past I would advise you to become one **now** because nature is nurturing for us humans physically, mentally, and spiritually.

You can be the first in your friendship group to instigate positive changes. Others will likely follow in your footsteps. Focus solely on the now and how you can be your best version currently, as this will help you to continually ascend into all forms of self improvement. Do not allow visions of the far future to cause you stress, because all you can control is your actions in the present, and this is what helps people to become more consistent.

I use a daily tasks to-do list to enable me to work through what I do have control over and get more done in my present day instead of stressing about the past or future.

Take it one day at a time and I guarantee that your predicted future will get much brighter.

No one can turn back the hands of time but what we can do is act now to create the circumstances we want to live in. Life is a blessing and I'm here to embrace every second of it through both happiness and hardships.

Right now is the most important moment. Do whatever gets you through and beyond difficulties. I sometimes drive to clear my mind or put myself in situations in the now that will help me to stop thinking about the past or the future. Be conscious of the power of the present moment.

PAST EXPERIENCES

The truth is that in the past, when you've felt weak, this will still play a role in who you are today by providing you with wisdom and experience. Just because you were weak during that difficulty doesn't mean you will be weak in the present. Older siblings are usually wiser because they gained wisdom through going through and overcoming hardships in their lives. Quite literally, the hardships we face help us to gain deeper understandings of life itself.

You have to ask yourself the question…

Where are you now?

We are no doubt a product of our past experiences, but we shouldn't become a prisoner to what we have been through. By reminding yourself of the turmoil you have endured, it will create ruins in your present feelings and emotions.

You will need to let go of past emotions attached to your experiences. **If you spend time living in the pain from past experiences then you will begin to be filled with negative emotions** continually from something that has already happened.

You will be spoiling the possibility of a positive day by dwelling on unpleasant past experiences. *Self reflection from past encounters to enhance your present* version is a tactic well needed to improve on our ways and respect how far we've come. Every battle you've been through you have survived, so don't be hard on yourself, instead be your own cheerleader and respect yourself before seeking respect from someone else.

You cannot bring past problems into a present moment and expect things to end well. You can't carry a lack of trust into a new relationship because your last partner was not loyal. This will only end in turmoil. Could you imagine meeting someone new and getting on well in the present moment but then they're judging you based on someone from their past doing them wrong? You and I both know that it won't last long, so don't let these things impact you or your loved ones. The past will damage your present moment if not catered to correctly. It sounds like such common sense, but when living out these moments, in reality it's hard to take a step back and notice when we get caught up in our feelings and emotions.

As humans, we subconsciously put defence mechanisms in place to protect ourselves, but when our subconscious has installed defence methods to protect us from the pain of the past, it begins to be of detriment to our futures. Then we have to actively try to remove these and become more aware of the positives that the current encounters can present to us, instead of having barriers in place from past problems.

It's important that you actively try to overcome what is constantly bothering you. You can do so by expressing yourself and vocalising what you feel within, as this can help you to understand why you feel the way you do and you will be able to release the voice within your head, because as you express it, you will be releasing the emotions.

Often we all spend time thinking within our heads and when this happens to me, I use writing down my thoughts as a tactic to help me analyse what the voice within my head is saying. It is good to be able to visually see on paper the thoughts you have been thinking. This helps me to notice when I haven't been thinking the way I want to and to understand that we are the being behind the voice in our heads and we don't always control what that voice is saying, but we need to acknowledge and counter attack when that voice is trying to put us down.

You can try to overcome past experiences by attempting to block or distract yourself from reliving memories that are hurtful. I usually wouldn't use this, but it can be effective at cancelling or limiting thoughts surrounding memories and experiences you would prefer not to remember. I normally try to feel then heal from issues, and remember the more you feel, the more you are connected with your inner self. Do not view sad emotions rising from the past solely as negative, because they can provide you with more understanding of yourself and life. This is exactly why I embrace instead of ignore the painful emotions I feel.

If you feel like you're in need of a change, then change the way you eat, change your routine, change absolutely anything you want to. It's good to experiment with different ways of living to find where you feel healthiest and happiest. Here's an example of how holding onto things from the past badly affects your present and future moments.

Imagine never driving a car again because of a crash you had 10 years prior. Do you see how that crash from the past has affected your daily life and future? If the **PTSD** of the past is left unattended to, then it will continue to affect your present and future. Take actions toward conquering your fears.

The person in the crash should sooner rather than later overcome the past trauma they faced and get back on the road driving again, for our past troubles shouldn't limit us cruising towards present progression.

Strength Over Length

Another aspect of past not present is to **never value the length over the strength** of a relationship. We are stuck in harmful ways at times. We feel like those we have known the longest would want the best for us but that's just not always the reality. Never, ever, value length over strength because why hold onto something from the past that's weaker and worse for you instead of enjoying and embracing the present relationship that is much stronger and more aligned with you?

A lot of couples today remain together because they've been together for a long time, but actually they may not be as compatible as they once thought or wished. The longer you stay with what's not meant for you, the longer you decline what is. What I mean by this is, how can a void be filled by a strong relationship if that void is filled with a weaker one? This applies to all forms of relationships. You could've met a new friend this year who has better intentions for your future than your 10 year long high school buddy. Relating back to 'KEEPING GOOD COMPANY', it's very important you keep good genuine people in your social group. Never let your loyalty to the wrong people hold you back from becoming your best version.

The strength is more important than the duration of a relationship. The strength is the present moment's condition of that relationship and the length is just a reflection of how long into the past you've known someone. Have you ever heard the saying people change like the weather?

Well I'm from London and the weather changes often. In life, we need to always bear in mind that people have their own issues and scenarios which need catering to, so we can't expect our loved ones and friends to always be there for us. However, when I state the strength over length concept, it is to reiterate that someone from the past who you have known much longer might be a weaker relationship than a new friend you met just this year. It's important you associate with like-minded people. You don't want to hold onto a friend from the past who continually dampens your dreams because they don't have any visions of future progressions for themselves.

The longer we keep what isn't for us from the past, the longer we block the present moment's blessings that can be bestowed upon us.

Let the past purify us for the present.

"Laa Ba'sa Tahoorun Insha'Allah"

The quote above in Arabic translates to:

Do not worry, it will be a purification (for you), God willing.

This quote resides with me very well, for I first read it inside prison and I interpreted it as all the hardships we face in life are there to purify us.

Did you know from a **chaotic beehive comes Purity?**

The beehive analogy that purity can be created from chaos came to me spontaneously whilst watching a documentary. It made me realise through times of chaos, we can develop and become our most pure version. You never truly know the strength you're made of until after going through adversity, so don't feel like the past problems were there to break you, because they very well could be a part of the ingredients to make you stronger.

EVERY single thing that has happened to us in the past can be used to help us develop.

When you start to view your losses as lessons, you learn so much more.

When you notice what you gain from your wounds, you become more wise.

When you realise that to progress you sometimes need to feel pain, then the pain is endured with a smile. Through all our troubles we need to learn to enhance ourselves for the present moment. For example, seeing my dad lifeless in his coffin box in the past makes me in this present moment enjoy the life I'm living regardless of my struggles or troubles and all the in-betweens. When we use our hardships as fuel we become undefeated.

After enduring a painful past, we also get to enjoy the better times with more appreciation and gratitude, because we have felt the difference.

Now how can a man who always has it good, feel how good that goodness is, if he has never felt what it's like to be without the good?

So keep in your mind that all the dark times help you appreciate the light.

All the difficult times help you to be grateful in times of ease. Each new day is a day of new beginnings. Live in the present moment. Tomorrow morning, when you wake up, think of your day as two blank pages waiting to be filled by your choices!

How are you going to fill today's pages?

Are you going to carry on the struggles of yesterday?

Or actively make decisions to better your ways?

Pondering on the past is harmful to your present day. Don't let today's goodness be snatched by past problems.

The sooner you live in the current moment, the sooner you will rebuke your future regrets. Many individuals realise at a later stage in their life, that we need to take daily action towards enjoying the present moment because our whole existence in the past and future could only exist by going through the present moments we're currently living in.

I used to live near a hospital that was close to the football pitches where my team played, when on my way back from football I used to take my time to speak to people sitting alone outside the hospital. Those were mostly elderly people who may not be with us anymore, but their advice still lives on within me. They taught me so much in terms of how to battle towards never feeling regret in the future, because they had regrets of their own. If you don't act now, you will feel that regret and when you do, it's impossible to go back and change the time we're currently living in. So act now to avoid your future self ever feeling regret. Live now in this present moment the life you've always wanted to live.

I wouldn't even let a negative Sunday impact my Monday, let alone allow the past to constantly plague me. That isn't just because it's the first day of the week either, we shouldn't allow any negative day to ruin our hopes of tomorrow or cancel our faith in the present.

Nothing lasts forever; the world's best footballers right now will eventually need to retire. Life goes on, so don't spend another day in the past when you can embrace the present. We need to avoid feeling regret in our lives and instead live in the now. Let's not be in denial of how important the present moment is to every single one of us and by living wholeheartedly in this very moment we will be limiting the potential regrets of the future.

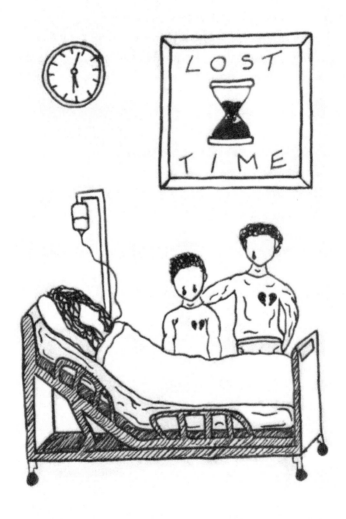

Artwork by Romario L.

7
REBUKE REGRET

"Don't do actions you'll live to regret, but take action right
now to do the things you may end up regretful of not doing."
- Sean Walsh

Regret...

We must live a life of rebuking regret, because more often
than not, we don't get a second chance at rectifying our
regrets. Especially because we mostly only realise what we
have had once it's lost or regret a moment in the past we
can't return to.

So take action in the present moment to rebuke your regrets
of tomorrow. Regret is so bitter that you'll only understand it
once you have felt it, but prevent having to feel regret by
living the life you've always wanted to live in this exact
moment.

The main goal in life is to be happy. Don't feel like you're
obliged to work the majority of your time; you have to keep in
mind that time cannot be returned to, so invest more time
into doing what you truly love and what results in more
happiness for you. This is easier said than done, because
when we have a family to support and bills to pay, it results in

us feeling obliged to work most of our days. Yet the reality is **we shouldn't sacrifice our happiness in the process of maintaining finances**, because what is a wallet full of cash in the pocket of an unhappy person? Maintain yourself, don't get into debt but don't chase truckloads of money and lose who you are in the process.

The times we are living in, we have people who devote their whole lives to money-making and then live a life of limited happiness due to chasing pay-checks. We attach our own self worth to the amount of finances we have accumulated. I know people that are rich financially but internally are empty and I know people who are just getting by but their hearts are full of happiness, love and purity.

I have been on both sides of the spectrum with this. There was a time as soon as I woke up, all I thought about was the next way I'm going to make money and although I gained finances, I genuinely lived a life of less passion and happiness. I didn't go out on weekends, I stopped my regular flights abroad, and I even avoided going on dates, all due to the pay check chase. There was a period when I sacrificed hobbies, family time, passions and even my own fitness in the process of money making. **However, gaining thousands whilst losing time with loved ones and quitting passions was a bad transaction.** Money is the means to support, not limit our living. Money shouldn't be our main priority because the chase will begin to deprive us of time with our loved ones and evades us from our passions. Only you have the power to create the change you envision. No one is going to come and make the adjustments for you, learn of the regrets of those before us and do not live out your days in ways you don't want to be living. You do have the time to make a difference. I would advise you to quit what you don't want to do and put all your effort into finding a job that you will feel passionate about. This will mean you can have the best of both worlds. **This is when passion and income become combined** and that's a gateway to a life of happiness. You will cancel out regrets of the future by working a job you love, and that's even if the pay is less, but it's very likely that with your passion injected into the work, you will gain more money, be happier and will be rebuking future regrets.

You don't need to look far to gain knowledge of possible regrets you could feel in the future. Ask an elder relative or even a stranger of the things they wish they didn't do or did do sooner. By accumulating the knowledge of possible regrets, you become more aware of aspects of life you need to avoid or take action towards. Regrets could be anything from mistakes made, letting thoughts plague your younger days, not enough action or even simply (but heartbreakingly) working so much that you missed your children growing up. Regrets are personal to each and every person but by learning of others' regrets, which they can't rectify, you can instil the needed awareness to take action towards living wholeheartedly in every moment and giving yourself the best chance at living a life full of passion, purpose and happiness. Always give yourself a try!

Don't regret not being your own cheerleader.

This isn't to be arrogant but to be confident in yourself. Many people regret not believing in themselves and by not having belief in themselves it has led them to live a life of doing the things they don't love. Once that time has passed, which it will, they will regret not taking action in their younger years. Many people find out who they truly loved in life after losing their lover.

You only regret not calling your grandparents often once they've passed away. Most regrets can't be rectified, so to stop these regrets harming the future you, live a life of rebuking regret. Live every single day wholeheartedly and do everything you love to do and more importantly make sure you create memories with loved ones because **memories are more valuable than money**. You never know when it's the last time you're going to see your friends or family. I know this through experience, the last time I saw my dad alive I would've never thought the next day he'd pass away, so don't regret not spending time with those you love. By choosing **memories over money,** your future self will be grateful not regretful, because money comes and goes but a moment in time can't be returned to.

I use this 12 week cycle to ensure I work hard but also travel as much as I'd at least like to. 12 weeks working, 1 week holiday, and this keeps me motivated whilst in work mode for with each week of hard graft, I'm a week closer to being on a beach, alongside palm trees, with sand between my feet. Memories over money at all times. Money is just a currency, so do not sell precious time for money which is spent so easily because time passed cannot be repurchased. What I mean by this is, missing out on a younger sibling's sports day for an extra day of pay, when that extra day of pay can be spent so easily, isn't worth it. The memories of you being present when your younger sibling wins their first ever race will be remembered forever. As will the look on their face seeing you there for that special moment. It is absolutely worth every hour invested to be there.

In fact, many extended family members should, along with both parents, try to be actively present in the lives of their siblings and children and choose to be present at as many moments as possible. That's because these times cannot be returned to. A father constantly working and not spending time with his children will in the future regret not spending more time with the kids during their childhood. Of course, we need to work, but it's about crafting a life for yourself which you won't regret in the future. What I'm questioning is, will

those extra hours at work for a few more thousand be worth missing out on memories of your kids' childhood?
I highly doubt it.
I wrote a quote of my own in 2019…

"When the day comes that you **can't** do what you **can,** is the day you wish you **could.**"- **Sean Atlas Walsh**

I got this quote tattooed on my chest just yesterday and it's quite ironic that whilst my ink is healing I can't go to the gym, and now that I can't exercise, I wish that I could. So make sure you do everything you can, whilst you can, because when you aren't able to, you're going to wish that you could.
I'll explain a situation regarding my good friend Sanchez. He tore his ACL and whilst injured not a single day passed that he didn't wish he could do what he used to be able to. Only now that he can't do what he could, he wishes he can, and this resulted in him having increased work ethic once he recovered, because he has now felt what it feels like to not be able to do what he once could. Meaning now that he can, he does so!
It's important we take action to bounce back from any mishap we experience. Our reactions are very important, as they determine the level of detriment an experience can have on us. With injuries, for example, do not let them be disheartening because you will regret not attempting to recover and build yourself back to your best.
One individual could get injured and end up quitting the sport they love and another individual could get the same injury and use that time to learn new techniques and ways to boost their recovery. As a result, the latter will bounce back to being stronger than they were before, both physically and mentally.
In life, adversity will happen, but do not become regretful for not taking action towards going and growing through each experience.

The Not So Common, Common Sense

Don't regret not taking action. Take action whilst you can, for you never know what the future holds for you.

Now, your interpretation of this quote is more important than my explanation because ask yourself... What is it that you absolutely **can** do but are not doing and one day you won't be able to do?

Do you visit elderly family members? Do you do what makes you happy?

What is it you're going to wish to be able to do when you can't do it anymore?

Whatever your answers are, I suggest you put active effort into doing more of those things.

When the day comes that you find yourself not being able to do what you once could, you're going to wish that you could do it again, so while you can, do all the things you want to do!

DO THEM!

I'll give an example of this.

Let's say you have family living in the same city you're living in, so you can easily visit them but you don't go as often as you'd like. Then they move abroad and now you see them once every 2 years. Now you can't just cross the city to see them, but you're wishing that you could... whilst you can do these things in the present moment, make sure you do them, for they will conquer regrets of the future, you'll live a life full of the memories and the good times you've always wanted. The day you can't do what you can do, is the day you wish you could.

Right now, in this very moment you could reach out to a loved one and keep in touch with them. Don't wait on showing love to your older siblings because at any given time it could be the last time you hear from them. Don't become regretful.

We are somehow taught that the mind is the most powerful tool and of course we most definitely need the mind on our side. It is very powerful but why at times do we associate the heart to weakness? As if feeling emotion or following your inner feelings is a bad thing?

I want to explain that we need to listen to our hearts more than our minds. **If our heartbeat stops we will lose our life, but if we lose our minds we are still alive but living at a disadvantage.** So let that truth express to you that following your heart is more important, and by always following your heart, you will not end up regretting a single thing because you followed your intuition.

Decisions

Your decisions are so important in life as you will begin to look like the decisions you make. Whether these decisions are positive, such as going to the gym and eating healthy, or if you decide to drink alcohol excessively and eat unhealthy foods constantly, you will end up looking like the choices you make and have made in the past. So to avoid being regretful, make the decisions that are of the best interest to the future you.

Kill the chances of being regretful by making the correct decisions because these decisions will literally affect your appearance.

I look back on photos of my parents and think of what could've been and how beautiful they were in their younger years, before they made mistakes. Then I think of what is and how my mum currently appears as a human zombie all as a consequence of her decision to try heroin for the first time. She is always beautiful in my eyes regardless, but due to her choices, she looks far worse than she would have, had she made better decisions.

In later life you will end up looking more like the decisions you have made than your genetic buildup.

If you decide to be healthy, then your appearance will reflect that.

Just as if you constantly choose to live unhealthily, your appearance will reflect your choices.

Genetics play a massive role, but our daily decisions in life will have much more of an impact on our lives and looks.

I know a person who is blessed with god-given genetics, but sadly his character lets him down. He eats badly and doesn't push himself to do much more than what he's required to. He has great genetics and is somewhat still in good shape even with living unhealthy for years on end, but I believe when the future arrives (as it will), he will end up regretting not pushing himself to achieve what he is at present very capable of achieving.

**"Do not allow your decisions today
to become your regrets of tomorrow!"**
-Sean Atlas Walsh

If you constantly do all you possibly can to better yourself, then this will have you at peace within. You will know you have always given your best. Even when a boxer loses, if he knows in his heart he gave it his all, then the loss will be less bitter to accept than if he made decisions leading up to his loss that assisted in his defeat. Simply give it your best and you will terminate potential regret. Try your best at all times and never allow self doubt to become your biggest mistake and regret.

You need to decide right now to choose to do what is of your best interest and take good care of yourself entirely. You should never become regretful of not taking more care of yourself, but sadly many individuals do feel this immense regret when health inflictions arise.

Prevention is always better than a cure. You shouldn't sacrifice yourself for others any longer because the reality is if you neglect yourself it is only a matter of time until you physically and mentally can't be of any good to others anyway. So if you truly want to be of aid to your loved ones, then take good care of yourself first and foremost as this will enable you to be able to help your companions even more. You will be setting a good example for your loved ones to follow. My friend Tommy has even gotten his parents into fitness.

As I mentioned previously of how discipline can only be enhanced, maintained, or ruined by our own decisions and actions; the same applies to future regrets because we can decide now to do everything we can to rebuke them.

Tomorrow is a new beginning for me because I am going to rebuke all possibilities of feeling regret in the future by immediately taking good care of myself physically, mentally and spiritually.

You need to attempt to always make the correct decisions, even in the face of negative emotions, because this will enable you to cancel actions you will end up regretting.

Why do good then end up ruining it in a moment of negativity?

To rebuke your regrets, you need to stop allowing your mind to control you in adversity, because you could be a very good-hearted person daily and do so much good for others, but in one moment of uncontrollable outburst you can ruin all the good you have done.

I will give you an analogy.

A painter who has spent hours using their skills and delicate touch to paint the perfect picture, in the eleventh hour during adversity in an act out of character, they throw paint all over the portrait.

The piece is now completely ruined after all the hours of skill and delicacy put into the creation, with one outburst, all the hours of good invested is now wasted.

Allow this to express that all the good we do can be ruined in an instant if we can't make the right decisions in adverse situations. Don't act out of character in adversity and then become regretful of your own actions. This is similar to what I mentioned with our tongues needing orchestration. It's the same with our actions. Think twice before making a decision to avoid being regretful in the future.

After an angry outburst, individuals often try to remind others of all the good they have done prior to the outburst, but as with the painting, it is hard to reverse the impact of your decisions.

Decide to do all the things you love. Write out a list of the things you want to do this year and never be shy to try something new.

"Life is a gift that will keep on giving when making the right decisions."
- Sean Atlas Walsh

Don't let the what ifs be Catastrophic

The reality we experience is a result of what we are conscious of, attempt your best to avoid overthinking the negative potential outcomes. Manifest better for yourself and walk in faith towards opportunities with no self doubt holding you back.

I know this through firsthand experience when I was going through mental difficulty. I was viewing things negatively all around me, and looking back now, I don't know how I survived such dark times. Everything lost colour, it was almost as if I was living in black and white. Even the flowers never had colour, and I was going through tough times in life.

Truly though, I don't regret anything about it, because it has enhanced my present version. I know how to look at all the smallest aspects of life with appreciation. Every single leaf on a tree possesses beauty. Don't regret the hardships you have been through, they can, if utilised correctly, enhance your life for the better. I used to see all the potential negative outcomes first, ascending from the worst to the best in that order, but this isn't good because then you will be acknowledging many mishaps that will never happen. Looking back on those times, I would prepare for the worst and then any other outcome would be better than anticipated, but this is detrimental to many aspects of life. Don't ponder on the worst possible circumstances because it could hinder you from ever beginning whatever it is that you envision. **The Human mind attempts to steer us towards comfort. Our ancestral instinct is survival, but we all want more than dormant lives! We need to live before we die!** Consciously choose that you don't want to ever feel regret in the future and this will lead you to live life more willingly in the present moment. For regrets of the past become regrets to those not taking action towards doing what they've always wanted.

It is far better to take a chance at a new path in life and get lost than to stick to the same route and then end up regretting the life you've lived. Don't overthink things, take action now whilst you can, towards living the life you've always wanted. **Don't let the what ifs become catastrophic.** Many people spend or spent their early 20s questioning everything and trying to live a calculated life of minimal risk. I think taking risks towards achieving the life you've always wanted is no risk at all. The biggest risk is living a calculated life that doesn't feel authentic and then becoming elderly and regretting all you have done. It's far better to go on an adventure through life as your true self than to live a life of facade or a life of the exact same routine and minimal meaning. Now, some people's authentic selves are working, even myself included, and I honestly get a headache if I ain't making progress in one way or another on a day-to-day basis; but it's about working toward something you really want to do, following your passions, and taking the risks towards building up a path you've trail-blazed.

I had a girlfriend in my late teens who was working in retail and she always wanted a boutique. I even offered to cover her losses in the first year because I really wanted her to just get started. **Don't let the what ifs be catastrophic,** because that boutique never opened. Always remember that taking risks towards living the life you've always wanted to live, is less of a risk than running the chance of being plagued by old-age regrets.

Everyone I know is growing old too quickly, which I believe they'll live to regret because we should live as much as we can. I don't believe we were born to work 48 weeks with 4 weeks of time for ourselves. I'm quite ambitious and I'm not stating you should stop working so much, but make sure you're living a life of hard work and enjoyment.

Everyone I know is growing old too quickly. Don't limit the enjoyment of your life by feeling like you're too grown up to try new things. You can do anything you want. Don't regret always waiting for the perfect time to do something, because many years will pass by without you doing what you intended.

Time is of the essence, but we have plenty of time left to create a life we will enjoy living.

If you're 40 years old, who says you ain't got 60 years left to live? You should never feel like you're too old to begin to lead the life you want to live; life is so beautiful and precious.

Ask yourself, will the '**what if'** possible outcomes you have been overthinking be as damaging as the future feelings of regret for not taking action?

Opportunities present themselves to be grasped by those willing to take advantage of them. With risk comes reward, but taking that leap towards something you have always wanted to do, is it really a risk at all?

What are you risking? By taking a chance and attempting something you have never done before, this is no risk at all. I view taking risks to gain the life I want to live as no risk at all, as I am cancelling out future regret by giving myself the best chance at success. How are you going to ever know how good your business idea would've been if you allowed the '**what ifs'** to conquer your action towards getting your plans underway? Quite simply try all new avenues and take a chance at new pathways. That way you will never feel regret in the future, for you always gave it your best attempt. Even if the plans don't go well, you can return back to doing what you were doing before, until another opportunity presents itself.

If you allow the '**what ifs'** to stop you from taking a leap towards doing something you have always wanted to, it will turn into "if only I had" and that's when the regret starts to sadden you. It's honestly so much better for you to give yourself a try at whatever it is you want to do, because if you continue to ponder on the what ifs and not take action, you will never know what could've happened. *Do not allow the what ifs to be catastrophic.*

We all have our own right to believe in whatever we want to right?

So why are we not choosing to believe in ourselves? This should be instinctive, but unfortunately it isn't. Purposefully and forcefully believe in yourself. **Don't let your biggest**

mistake be not having faith in yourself because that will become your biggest regret.

A great warrior once burned the ships that he sailed to battle on, to eliminate all thoughts and possibilities of doubt or retreat, leading to his soldiers entering battle knowing it is either to live or to die. Now in our lives we won't face scenarios as serious as this, but you will definitely need to have more courage and take a leap of faith towards your desires!

Individuals who guide their thoughts away from overthinking many different outcomes and attempt to limit their fears; it's these people that change from a worrisome person to an individual of hope. Instead of being fearful due to negative overthinking, they become courageous by always taking action in the present moment. It's important you do this because the what ifs that are holding you back from becoming who you want to be, I'm sure these will feel less adverse than the emotion and feeling of deep regret that you risk by not taking action.

If you allow time to examine the what if outcomes, you will be instilling fear of things which have not yet happened. This is sapping yourself of your own strengths. If the lion spent time thinking of all the potential bigger beasts of the jungle, then the lion would be perceived as less fearsome.

In life, too many people seek a safety net and this could be the reason for their failures or the reason they have never truly lived.

Imagine the emotion of regret you will feel after living a life of limitations.

Don't fish in a pond if you have the abilities to fish in the sea, and don't live a life limited by the potential what ifs. Just take action and discover your abilities.

It's impossible to go back in time, we all know that, but there is one way we can change the past…

You see, Tomorrow will soon be Today, and Today will soon be Yesterday.

The regrets of yesterday we can't change unfortunately, but do not allow yourself to regret today when tomorrow arrives. The only way we can change the soon-to-be past, is by acting in the present moment, because with every second that goes by we are moving past times that we can never go back to. So take active action towards cancelling out potential regrets.

REBUKE REGRET at every chance you get. Slow steps towards doing what you've always wanted to do is better than no steps at all. So ask yourself:

Do you want to be regretful?

How in the future will you ensure you won't feel so?

By following this:

"Don't do actions you'll live to regret, but take action right now to do the things you may end up regretful of not doing." - Sean Walsh

Now, I always like to uplift people through positivity, but I also have to mention something that is a reality, death.

DEATH

Last week, on my way to get my tattoo, I drove past a graveyard and a thought struck my mind. If we were all slightly more conscious of death, would we live our lives better? I think we would.

Death shouldn't be perceived as negative at all, it is a part of life. Don't let death scare you. We will all pass away and hopefully do so painlessly, but use the thought of leaving this world behind to assist you in living life in any which way you want to!

It's your life, so do what suits you, and don't regret the life you have lived once time has passed.

We need to try to be conscious of the fact that our time is limited on this beautiful planet because to heal from our internal non-reality, overthinking thoughts, and difficulties, we need to notice and embrace the reality of what life really is. So when we **acknowledge that time is limited but not our existence,** then we can learn to utilise time more wisely and live the life we've always wanted. To be connected with nature is a blessing because you get to scc life for its true purpose and meaning.

Death is scary, but never fear death, because if you are a believer in god then death is literally your ticket to heaven. If you are spiritual, then death could be your ascendancy to another dimension...

Don't fear death and fail to live in the process.

Death is certain for each and every living entity on this planet, so why allow that certainty to halt your existence in this very moment or sadden your soul?

Even if you don't believe in god and you aren't spiritual, then you may believe after death there is nothing at all. So then why fear nothing or the end of life if it simply finishes completely?

You allow the fear of the unknown to bother you, but if you knew all that was going to occur, it would likely bother you more. **Imagine you knew the exact amount of days you have left to live... that's more frightening than not knowing, so don't fear the unknown because it actually could be providing you with more comfort than if you knew it all.**

I have met many individuals who fear death and try to not ever consciously think of it, as a tactic to be blissful in ignorance. This is completely fine, but I don't *force* myself to be reminded of death. Death is one of my biggest motivators because I know one day I won't be able to wake up on this planet and do the things I love doing. This gives me that extra push to live in the ways I want, whilst I'm alive.

Rebukc all possible feelings of regret in the future by doing whatever you want to and living life to your full potential at this very moment. Those young adults who fear death need to remind themselves that when in old age you may be much more receptive to the idea of passing away. This could be a result of wisdom or after years of enduring medical suffering, but I feel those who are elderly that I knew who have passed on, were much less fearful of death than the young adults, even though their time to move on was much closer.

This is exactly why it is more important to spend your time more wisely than your money…

Money comes and goes but time cannot be returned to. Don't be too frugal and then regret not treating yourself to better things. Do you think any person has grabbed their wallet when in their last breath?

The moment of today will soon be a memory. Do not dwell on yesterday and do not allow the pressure of the future to stress you. We have power over our present and can decide to make it as beneficial to us as possible. Always be yourself, you shouldn't waste time attempting to please strangers. No one can tell you how to be in this world, so don't end up regretting time wasted on trying to please everyone else.

On the 12th of March 2023, I had a weird moment where I felt like I had to consciously breathe. Breathing didn't feel second nature to me in that moment. It was frightening and in that very moment I thought to myself how genuinely precious life is. At any given moment we can experience our last breath. So be good to one another, don't be shy to express compassion, and live every single second of your existence to the maximum.

Another reason I mentioned death is because a lot of regrets come from the feeling of losing someone. For example, a fallout with a friend or family member, do not be shy to **forgive.**

Forgive them as soon as possible because you never know what tomorrow holds. The sooner you forgive one another, the sooner you can get back to making memories and having good times together. Fall outs in families are very common, but blood is thicker than water. Don't be stubborn and hold a grudge, reach out and sort it all out for you never know when it's someone's last day on the planet and regret is the saddest of all feelings.

Listen to your heart more closely and not your mind. Your mind is a tool that can be sharpened to help assist you through life, but your heart gets full-on emotions and feelings. Listen to your heart and follow the intuition you feel within, then conquer all possible regrets.

What will result in death quicker? Losing your heartbeat or losing your mind?

The answer will reveal to you the importance of following your heart in life. By always following your heart, you not only live a life that is much more genuine to yourself, but you also limit acknowledging and giving power to the mind that can harm you with overwhelming thoughts.

Follow your heart. We inherit stigmas through early life and many of us believe that the heart leads us to weakness. So I ask, isn't it in the heart where a mother feels the instantaneous love for her children?

Isn't it the heart that beats continuously to keep us living? We have to reconnect and then follow our hearts and by doing so you'll be rebuking regret!

You want to be positive right?

So why allow your mind to overthink negatively?

If you were sunbathing with the purpose of getting a tan, then the clouds covered all the sunlight and the sun went down, would you continue to lay there overnight still seeking a tan? No.

So why if you seek positivity do you allow yourself to overthink negatively? We have to have this battle within. Whenever we feel self doubt or overthink negative circumstances, you need to direct your mind in a better direction. You will need to forcefully cancel out negative thinking. Just as you will not get a tan under the moonlight, that's exactly how you will not become positive by allowing yourself to ponder on negativity.

"Don't wait for regret, rather live a life of memories you'll never forget."

-*Sean Atlas Walsh*

Artwork by Romario L.

8

SEEK SOLACE IN FAMILY AND FRIENDS

One of the most important parts of this book is about seeking solace in loved ones in times of difficulty. This could make a dark day seem just a little bit brighter and one small light in a room of darkness can make all the difference.

Firstly, I want to highlight how it is a strength to show emotion and absolutely not a weakness. I know in recent times the stigmas surrounding mental health have been changing but that doesn't mean the previous and newly created stigmas aren't affecting people. So never feel like being emotional is a weakness, it is perfectly normal both men and women have their share of feminine and masculine energy. By helping change the stigmas we can encourage people suffering in silence to open up and then alleviate their stresses. By doing so, we can heal those inflicted by mental ill health to live a better quality of life and prevent the loss of life to the sadness of suicide.

Life is like a rollercoaster, without the lows, the highs wouldn't feel as good. If the roller-coaster track was straight it wouldn't be as thrilling. We have to accept and become aware that the hardships we experience ultimately lead us to appreciate the highs and good times with more gratitude. Keep this in mind next time you feel down and it could alleviate some of the stress. You are humanly perfect when feeling the rollercoaster of life, and as with a rollercoaster, when it's going down at speed, it's to gain momentum for reaching higher heights. The hard times could be the fuel you need to push for something better, but it all starts from within. You won't get internal happiness seeking external things. The truly rich person is the one who is always grateful and content.

It's of utmost importance that in times of turmoil you seek solace in family and friends because by sharing your problems and feelings, it can halve the weight of your burdens. It's the same way when you need help carrying in shopping bags, you call on your family to halve the weight by simply having them help you. It's easier doing it together than doing it alone and the same applies to mental burdens, as well as physical. Be comfortable with family and friends, for you will find consolation in them during difficulty. It will also encourage your loved ones to be open to you in their times of need and you can all be there for one another.

Be honest with the ways you're feeling because only then can a friend or sibling completely understand what you're actually experiencing. Kids cry out loudly when they need something or aren't happy, babies express their feelings through cries and when constantly crying the baby then gets more attention and care from the parents. We shouldn't feel like we can't express ourselves amongst loved ones when we feel we are in need of help or in need of close attention. You won't need to cry out loudly but absolutely find solace in friends and family.

It's good to open up to those who care for you because the average person will not be able to notice their own errors or the root causes of their problems, so it is wise to communicate with those who want the best for you on how you can improve your ways and cancel making continuous errors.

Those within your family and friendship groups will want the best for you, so it's wise to ask them for advice because they will be able to express things from their own point of view. **Correction isn't rejection**. Do not have too much pride to ask for help from those you love.

Excessive amounts of pride will lead you to a life of limited understanding.

Open up your heart to your companions; this will help your mind to heal because without having an open heart and being entirely honest, your mind will not entirely absorb the help that your loved ones want to provide you with. The same applies to your mind. You must be open minded when giving and receiving help from others because we can all learn from each other on how to cope or ways to offload negative thoughts and emotions.

If you feel like you can't completely open up to family with your problems due to social, religious or any other reasons, then you will definitely benefit from attending a self-help group with others who are facing similar challenges and difficulties as yourself.

This will help you to become much more aware of other people's techniques and methods of alleviating burdens and forms of stress. It is wise to learn and become aware of other individuals' outlooks on life.

I wouldn't want anyone I know suffering in silence, so by opening up yourself it can actually give loved ones the confidence to express themselves freely.

Being open to loved ones can help shine some light in sad times and can also give you more insight on your issues for you to get an opinion from a different point of view regarding what's bothering you. More often than not, these different points of views on your troubles help enhance your strength and resistance towards them. That's because when going through tough times it's hard to view things from a different point of view when you are preoccupied with problems. Think of a heartbroken teenager after their first big break up. By speaking with their parents, they hear of their experiences and it gives them insight that it's normal to feel the way they're feeling. **Alleviation!**

Do not put too much pressure on your children, parents or friends…

We need to alleviate them from the pressures of the real world by providing comfort to them and helping them feel at peace when at home or in our presence.

Unlock the Love

Unlock the love within your family and friendship groups. It takes just one person to instigate showing affection to unlock the expressions amongst loved ones.

Many of our older siblings were raised in tough love ways by their parents, in which now they follow in those lack-of-affection footsteps. Many families live like this, so be the one courageous enough to say " I love you" to family and friends. You never know when you will last see someone and these 3 words can boost a companion's mood massively. I always express my love for friends and family.

Why do we find it so hard at times to express love to our family and friends?

Why does it feel awkward or difficult to say I love you to a sibling or friend?

When I was in prison my companions and I expressed ourselves more openly due to the circumstances I was living in, but we shouldn't have to go through trials or troubles to begin to be expressive to those we love.

We need to begin at once to unlock the love amongst our friends and family.

Even just some simple words of encouragement will have a massive impact on anyone, even strangers. **A little reassurance can never be underestimated.**

All small actions of love are important. Little notes left on the table for your partner to read as a short sentence of expression can make someone feel appreciated. Help boost the confidence of your loved ones, as all small actions or gestures for your companions will go a long way. I sometimes wait until 11:11 am to say good morning to my sisters because I know they're conscious of numbers and view them as spiritual signs for a bright day.

You can even radiate positivity towards strangers in a world full of negativity.

I know so many people who have such broken relationships with their family members and my family is no different, but where does it begin to go wrong?

Be kind to one another and put effort into being there for each other. Life isn't always easy. Be humble if you haven't yet experienced difficulties and be close to your loved ones as it will help you through tough times.

If someone close to you is experiencing any form of mental ill health, simply just be there for them and listen to them patiently. Do not rush them through their explanation when they begin to open up, instead make them feel worthy of every second of your time and comfort them.

Our small actions play a massive role in helping someone feel welcomed and to feel safe enough to express their issues. If someone is being open with you and you begin to rush them, how do you think that will make them feel?

Put yourself in their position. You will feel as if what you're saying doesn't mean much to them, so be patient when listening to loved ones' problems.

We have to take into account that those suffering with mental illnesses do not choose to feel the way they feel. Do not be tough on them and make them feel as if it's entirely their fault, because mental ill health isn't always due to the actions of the person inflicted; the circumstances they are facing could be no fault of their own but be the cause of their suffering.

Comfort your loved ones as much as possible.

A random hug can boost a companion's feelings massively. A text to check up on friends can make them feel like they mean something and are worthy.

Don't be distant from those who care for you, as all your loved ones would rather be there for you than to have you suffer in silence.

The sanctuary you've always needed has been right next to you the whole time and you find that sanctuary in opening up to friends and family.

We are naturally social beings, although occasional solitude is good for your spirituality, being in contact with loved ones can be crucial to your mental stability. When spending too much time alone you can actually start to believe thoughts that aren't reality.

The help you may need could simply be in a companion you trust.

Opening up to one another is also good because it will strengthen the relationship in many ways. The love is more deep rooted after uplifting one another. Some friends will only be there through the best of times, but the friends who are there always, they become family. Those friendships are irreplaceable and irrefutable. Remember there are things in this life money can't buy and loyalty is one of them, so count yourself rich if you have a loyal friend or family member.

In life, when we experience things, we often get the urge to speak to someone about it.

Whether positive or negative, we feel like sharing our experiences, but we should only speak to friends and family regarding personal matters. **Even positive things are best to be kept private.** Don't share all emotions and occurrences with everyone because 'Residents of Evil' are there waiting to locate your soft spots to know how to get to you and positive scenarios can harvest jealousy in those who don't love you. In many cases, when opening up to the majority of people, you'll be left feeling more anxiety because then you've made people aware of your issues that need solving. It is best kept within the sanctuary of family and friends. True solace will be found amongst them. Consolation with loved ones will leave you with advice that's of your best interest and more importantly you won't feel badly judged for your problems.

It is very important to unblock and release feelings, thoughts and emotions because bottling them deep within you will be harmful and result in physical, mental and spiritual energy being exerted on trying to hold a facade appearance when really you are deeply hurting.

Opening up leads to a better quality of life because you can come to terms with the grief you're facing, and rather than dwelling on current and past experiences, you can heal and move forward.

Suppressing your thoughts and emotions within yourself can be likened to an apple which appears perfectly edible on the outside but is really rotting to its core.

Rid yourself of the inner demons and with the help of those dear to you, defeat those negative internal feelings. Let go of the heavy emotional backpack that is weighing on your heart and soul. As with the shopping bag example, cut your stress in half with the help of others. It isn't a weakness to need a shoulder to lean on at times.

I once heard some elderly Irish folk in a pub saying,

"Pain passes through families until it's ready to be felt."

I couldn't agree more with what I heard, do not allow the hardships of the past to impact your friends or family perpetually. Feel the feelings, embrace the hardships, open up to one another, get comfortable expressing your emotions to each other and heal together. This is what family and friends are there for. Don't let anyone suffer in silence due to a stigmatised opinion.

We need to defeat all stigmas surrounding mental illness and by doing so we will be saving the lives of those suffering in silence resulting in suicide.

Unconditional Love

It is easy to love someone when they do things for you, when they're nothing but bearers of positivity and when they support you in every way possible.

If you only love someone in these circumstances and for the benefits they bring, then the love you have for them is conditional. All love is good love but in a world full of constant changes and troubles, unconditional love is the best form of love to have with someone.

It is easy to be happy and maintain a relationship with a friend or family member when everything is going well but **when adversity hits, those who are conditional will vanish.** This is exactly how people who have been through difficulty have less friends, because they have discovered who is truly there for them regardless of their situation. Relationships that grow through what they go through become the most genuine, the most full of love and the most understanding. There will be no better feeling than celebrating when good times arise with those who stuck by you in times of trials and tribulations. These are the companions who are truly deserving of your efforts and time. Sweetness tastes more sweet when you have been eating sour, just as good times will feel extremely good after enduring difficulties together.

The good thing about not always having it easy is that you will have no doubt about who truly is your unconditional friends and family members.

The love grows stronger after going through good and bad times together, as love can be lost in an instant if an individual doesn't stand by you through turmoil. **Imagine** the intense love a prisoner will have for a woman who waited for him and remained loyal. She would be worth changing one's lifestyle for. **Imagine** how nice it would be to become financially successful with friends who stuck by you in times of need!

There will be no better feeling than to become a success with those who you have struggled with.

The next time you're faced with challenges in life, look up and notice who is still around to help you and those who are there for you are the individuals who love you unconditionally. Through difficulties we can acknowledge our truest friends and family.

Unconditional love is a two way transaction so be there for your family and friends who need you during their adversity, as well. Even simply opening an ear, listening to their problems, and giving some advice can enhance a relationship from casual to unconditional.

We shouldn't only be friends with people for potential benefits. This is exactly how successful individuals struggle to determine when someone is genuine or when someone has their own interest at heart or ill intentions.

Unconditional friendships have no terms and conditions to thrive and be maintained. This is the purest form of a relationship with someone because it will be maintained regardless of circumstance.

NOW

Don't feel bad when unfriending someone who you are certain is a conditional friend.

Do not spend time or energy feeling like you need to uphold friendships which have shown themselves to be conditional. I am too self aware to be a bad person, but with removing conditional friendships you shouldn't feel bad about deserting them because these friends or family only surround you when things are going well. As a result of removing them, I can invest my time, energy and support to those who are unconditional instead.

Unconditional love can be found even after years of longing for a partner who will keep you company and alleviate all of your worries. This is why you hear so many love songs on the radio, because love can bring you peace and give you the strength you need to overcome anything that life throws at you.

It's very important we create a loving atmosphere for our family and friends, as this will help assist not only others, but ourselves through tough times. I know it isn't always perfect at home and personalities of family and friends can clash at times, but even if you ain't getting along, you wouldn't want anything bad happening to a loved one. Look out for them and don't be stubborn after arguments, because it could lead to years of not talking.

I have lived 12 years of my 24 year life with my brothers and sisters and I have spent the other 12 almost 13 years living away from them. I know the experience of being with and without family and also with and without a family home.

Through all the trials and tribulations we have to unconditionally love our true family and friends and actively be there for them.

Suicide

The saddest way for a soul to leave this planet is by their own choice to terminate their life due to the constant pain they're feeling. According to World Health Organisation, approximately 800,000 people pass away annually due to suicide.

I believe we all need to attempt to prevent such sad happenings from occurring. Take a second to comprehend the amount of souls who have felt so low in this world that they didn't even want to be here anymore.

Suicide has a massive ripple effect on the family and friends of the individual who has taken their own life as well. It isn't the end of the pain because everyone who cares for someone who has passed away, well that's when their deepest sorrows begin. So by preventing suicide, we are actually preventing so much suffering, even more than the one person we are helping.

How would you feel if you lost a close companion to suicide? Look out for your loved ones as much as possible and burst the stigma that surrounds us humans about being open and honest in how we are feeling. It isn't a weakness at all to admit and accept the ways you feel.

If you see anyone seemingly very distressed and upset, be of help to them because at times people who feel suicidal feel like they can't open up to the people they know. You could be the stranger that saves them and guides them in their lowest of lows.

We have to be here for each other because it's a tough world as it is, without all the stigmas surrounding the ways we feel, and how we feel pressured to live.

As I write this I have just passed my exams on mental health awareness and I will soon be enrolling to study counselling and neuroscience. My life will be well spent if I spend it with the purpose of helping others.

In a world which is so fast paced and ruthless, it is good to become someone who is passionate in regard to helping others. **No one is perfect, but your imperfections could provide you with the experience required to help others overcome their personal challenges.** If yourself or anyone you know has had thoughts of suicide, reach out and seek help. There is no shame in working on improving your mental state and returning back to your best feeling version.

I would rather listen for months on end to a friend's problems than to hear of them passing away from suicide. When I was younger and I used to hear of people who were suicidal, in my naïve ways,

I used to get frustrated because I thought to myself that my dad would love to live for a single minute longer, but as I've gotten older I understand it completely. We need to become more aware of suicide and the fact we all hurt at times. Although in those moments it may not feel like it; life is a true blessing to be alive.

Suicide is preventable, no one is beyond receiving help. There is so much that can be done to stop such sad circumstances from taking place.

We have to try to reach out and check on our close companions as much as we can. I have seen and heard too many scenarios of nobody having a single ounce of suspicion of the beautiful soul lost to suicide's issues until it's sadly too late.

We NEED to ensure our loved ones are doing well and by finding solace in one another we do just that. You can cancel out people suffering in silence in your family and friendship groups by being the first person to be outspoken regarding mental instability, especially because it is highly stigmatised and discriminated against in different religions, cultures and societies.

In the UK, suicide is the leading cause of death in people aged between 15-24 years old and the biggest killer of men under 49 years old. To read such statistics breaks my heart because being someone who is empathetic and after going through all the hardships I've gone through and the tough times I've endured, I can understand how someone can lose hope in this world we are living in. Ultimately we need to remind ourselves, alongside everyone, that everything and any circumstance can change as long as you give it a genuine chance to.

I now use spontaneous action to conquer the days where I feel at my lowest. It's the best way to shake up your existence and you can spontaneously discover something you love to do whilst distracting yourself from your burdens. This is a tactic to use when you feel stress is getting the better of you. Still, on a day to day basis, try to identify and understand why you feel the way you do at intervals. Then go back to being your own mental pilot and fly yourself to where you best feel.

In your saddest moments, never ever feel like you can't reach out to anyone. If you want a private chat and to confide in someone where you won't feel judged, there are helplines in which you have access to 24 hours a day, 7 days a week. (I will provide the helpline numbers in the back of this book) As I write this, only 2 days ago have I heard the terrible news regarding another young man who shared the same school as me having passed away to suicide. Helping prevent suicide is one of my main purposes in life, even when I was in prison a fellow prisoner hung himself due to the pressure of his sentencing. I wish I was there before he tied the rope to help his way of thinking and after these scenarios of sorrow I feel the need to do everything I can to help prevent such sad tragedies from happening. Always keep in mind that bad weather passes and clear skies will follow. After enduring dark times, even normal times feel extra good, keep in mind when you're at the bottom, truly the only way is up!

You genuinely never know how your words can impact and help a person.

I have an elderly friend, who in god's honest truth had a problem with drug abuse and was drinking large amounts of alcohol. One day we were having a discussion about life and its meaning, then I briefly told him that after my dad's accidental drug overdose, not a day goes by that I don't miss him and I would give anything to see him again. I told him how at least twice a month I pay his grave a visit, and then by opening up and sharing our thoughts, little did I know one part of our conversation that night would help save my friend's life. Because when he found himself at the bottom of the bottle and alone in the darkness of his thoughts, he was extremely upset and was going to attempt taking his own life, due to being fed up with his life's circumstances and going around in circles. He had a feeling of no purpose, and in the very moments leading up to him attempting to take his own life, he made no one aware of it, as he felt he had no one to confide in. Yet in that very moment during his lowest of low, a small section of our conversation came to his mind and prevented him from going forward and taking the actions which could've killed him. I felt so humbled when he told me about this because to know just by having that conversation and opening up to each other, it could be the very reason he's still with us and now he's doing very well for himself as he has gone on to travel and build a life for himself in Thailand. When we occasionally FaceTime now he always reminds me that my words have an impact in ways that my unpretentious self couldn't imagine, but really I'm just grateful that he's still alive and breathing.

Allow this to show you that one conversation with friends or family members could be the conversation to uplift them beyond their stresses and install belief in themselves. But more importantly, that life is worth living because times are always changing.

If you are on your highest of heights at the moment, don't look down upon anyone because your consciousness might not even be able to comprehend how another person is feeling. Don't judge people all the time for their actions, at times adversity gets the better of all of us, whether rich, poor, strong or weak, we are all human beings with emotions, thoughts and feelings.

Just because someone is poor, that doesn't mean they're unhappy and just because someone is rich, doesn't mean they're immune to feeling the lowest depths of sadness.

My cousin in Ireland had a friend who was very popular, young, talented and had his whole life ahead of him. I met him on a visit to the homeland and he was a good person. I would've never imagined this person to pass away from the sadness of suicide, so ensure you have heart-to-hearts with your close ones, because you never know how someone is feeling behind closed doors. Let's try our best at saving as many people from suicide as much as possible. This is a topic we need to learn about from past scenarios and stop it from reoccurring to others in the future.

Mental health is unique in terms of each and every person feeling unique to themselves and can be affected by things that are personal to them.

An individual could have gone through something a thousand-fold easier, but feel a thousand times worse than someone who's genuinely had it rough. For example: Someone who suffers from severe anxiety will feel overwhelmingly stressed and under pressure while speaking to a group of 5 people, but someone else who is speaking to 50,000 people may feel comfortable in public speaking and being judged doesn't even cross their conscience. So remember that mental health is unique to each and every person.

You shouldn't feel judged for any which way you're feeling, but it's important you be true to yourself, as anything forced loses its authenticity. If you don't feel religious you shouldn't be forced to follow a path that isn't aligned with you, but to millions and millions of people religion offers life a purpose. As I said with passion-pursuing, find what's authentically you and do more of what makes you happy and you will mentally feel at your best.

Never judge someone for stressing over something you view as minute just because that's what personally stresses them out. They may have strengths over the things you stress, so seek solace in family and friends and gain perspective on life from the viewpoint of yourself and others.

Some families have the finances or network to send a sibling abroad when facing a mental breakdown. I know a family who sent their teenage sons back to Somalia because they were getting into trouble in London and that experience in their homeland completely changed them.

I know another individual who was having difficulty with alcohol and drugs and decided he was going to go live with family on the other side of the globe and by doing so he made a full recovery and no longer has issues with substance abuse. What about the families who don't have the financial means to do such things?

This is why it is of lofty importance to create a sanctuary in the home you live in. Create a comfortable atmosphere where all your siblings feel they can seek solace and not feel further judged by doing so.

Lead by example.

Be the companion who is the first to open up on their thoughts and feelings. It is much harder for younger siblings to express their struggles first. No one wants to be seen or portrayed as weak or a victim, but this is of more importance than any stigmatised opinion. This is being true to yourself and your most inner feelings, then sharing them with others to halve your burdens. By doing this you will be leading by example; portraying the courage to admit your adversities. Let's be open, honest and work towards helping one another at all times, not just in our darkest moments. Find the warmth of the sanctuary you have in family and friends and then keep the fire burning.

Lead by example to your younger family and friends. You can't be demanding your siblings to work harder when you don't work hard yourself. The same way if you don't open up and be honest with your siblings it may make them not want to be open with you. To cancel out having loved ones suffering in silence, we need to lead by example and open ourselves up first. We can learn from one another to aid us through and beyond mishaps, stresses and struggles.

Every person has their own unique point of view, their very own outlook on life, and this is exactly why it is good to communicate and be open completely with close companions in conversation. You can learn of so many different points of view and understand many different perspectives from those who genuinely want the best for you.

Every two pupils have their own viewpoint, just as every mind has its own unique perspective on life.

As you are improving
And you are improving,
You'll begin to notice.

Artwork by Isabella P.

9
THE POWER OF PERSPECTIVES

The beautiful power of perspectives can help you feel different within an instant, for the way we view things is crucial to our inner feelings and ultimately our viewpoint on life is the first starting point of how all things affect us. If you're aiming the arrow in the wrong direction it will not land on target, so if you target a life of happiness, then alter your perspective in the right direction to increase not only your happiness but also your resilience and understanding in life. After altering your perspective you'll begin to notice aspects of life you have never noticed before. There is so much to appreciate when you look deeply into things.

Some people consider themselves born with genetic strengths in certain departments, but these strengths are all a consequence of our conscious and subconscious perspectives.

The power of perspectives will impact us whether we notice the impacts or not.

For example:

This very paper you're reading these words on was once a part of a tree. With a positive perspective in life, you will enhance all positives around you. **You will have more gratitude than ever before, for you will notice all the smaller things to be grateful of and you will also overcome negatives, because your perspective will increase your understanding.** You will look at life overall from a better viewpoint. As with me in my prison cell, I could've noticed the four pain-scratched walls, locked door, floor and ceiling, but instead I appreciated the small gap in the window so I could enjoy the little glimpses of nature. If I, myself, can make my time in a smelly cell more pleasant with the power of perspectives, then you as my reader can most definitely create a life more pleasant with an altering of your perspective.

Living this way since I was young has helped me view every test in life as a blessing because it's never truly a loss if you learned a lesson. It can help you change your wounds to wisdom, pain into progress and get fuel from negative emotions which can be utilised to make you a better version. I'll give you an example of how I have altered a perspective to instantly conquer or limit sadness:

The day my grandfather passed away was very sad, and I will always be grateful to the man who was a good father to my father and a great grandfather to me, may George Walsh rest in peace. When he passed away, instead of me drowning in my tears like I normally would, I altered my perspective from viewing him as dead, to the fact that now he's simply at rest. This didn't stop all the tears because I still shed buckets loads, but it did limit the sadness of his passing because I know now my granddad no longer has to take daily medicine and doesn't have to endure struggling to breathe. He isn't suffering and now he doesn't have to feel the pain of missing his firstborn son (my father) or Nanny Noreen anymore because he will be in heaven with them. Just by a change of perspective I kept myself positive and it made me accept something heartbreaking with more resilience.

The power of perspectives can help you get over the toughest tests in life by becoming aware of how troubles can assist your triumphs after experiencing them.

In life, if you only ever view your tough times as bad times of no benefit, then that is all they will consciously be. I want to help people understand a little further that our bad experiences have benefitted us openly and subconsciously. The **trouble to triumph** perspective will help you to acknowledge this.

An example is, an individual who has had a very bad childhood will know how to be a better parent to their children because the troubled individual will put extra effort into ensuring their children have a better childhood than they had. This will also enhance their drive to live a better adult life for themselves after a troubled childhood.

My older sister Sinead has raised her children absolutely perfectly, in every way, even down to the point she was blending vegetables so that her children had healthy food with nutrition and so that they could eat the vegetables they didn't like the looks of. She also, at the young age of 21, became the full time carer of my little sister Siobhan. I am a very proud younger and older brother of the women they have become, and I know my dad would be proud from beyond.

Our tough times enhance us for our futures, just like the hard gym sessions that increase your strength.

With my older cousin Richard, his father wasn't present throughout his life and now he is a great father to his daughter. There is no sacrifice he wouldn't make for her, for you see in life the tough times can teach us good morals and empathy through experience, so precisely by not having good parents, this can lead you to be a better parent yourself.

Troubles improve us in mysterious ways. We sometimes won't even notice our improvements because they happen organically like trees growing stronger after enduring the cold winters, strong winds, and storms; which then makes the roots grow more firmly into the soil and the stormy clouds provide the water they require to grow.

It is so uplifting to view the gains instead of the pains of the past. You can do so by always focusing on gaining strength and resilience from each and every experience.

The power of perspectives can be utilised and be very effective at noticing the good counterparts to each past trouble. This can help you to overcome traumas of the past or stop you from holding onto bad emotions. For example: **A relationship** that has now ended with your previous partner, instead of being bitter about it not working out, have the perspective that you both gave the relationship the best chance, tried your best, and maybe it is for both of your best interests to part ways. After going through difficulty and then a break up, you will also learn of the traits and characteristics you don't want in your future other half, leading you to have a better understanding of who to date in the future.

After overcoming heartbreak certain music sounds better as well, for you can relate to the lyrics, literally turning pain into pleasure.

Loss of freedom will make a person appreciate being free because the person will now empirically know the difference between having freedom or not. Before you lose something that you have always had, how are you meant to fully understand what you've got?

So again, when we go through things we gain insight.

Transgressions could be the ingredients to fuel your progression or to simply help you live life with more appreciation.

The death of a family member will make the family cherish time more dearly. It can bring distant family members back into contact after the loss and hardship. After the loss of a loved one we can learn to live each day more positively and learn to be grateful that we are still breathing.

A bad injury and time out from training to heal can make you train harder and smarter than ever before. Ask someone who has had to have time away from a passion they love, how they felt. I'm sure not being able to do what they once could will make them re-appreciate being able to do so again.

This perspective can be applied to so many different aspects of life to acknowledge the gain instead of the pain of past happenings.

One personal part of my life I improved by using the power of perspective was when I changed my perspective on my parents' addiction to heroin. The new perspective instantaneously changed my feelings towards what was once one of my greatest sorrows.

After years of begging them to stop, I changed my perspective from a powerless position of nothing will help them and that they were like two zombies needing opium, to a perspective of understanding their needs and that potentially anytime they were high they were completely relaxed and stress free. Whether this was true or not, the perspective change massively impacted my feelings regarding their addiction. It limited the sadness of my mother's still existing addiction and I now think of the situation as when she's high she's happier and she's numb to the world and all of its worries.

Your perspective is so pivotal in regard to how anything affects you.

Another way I used a shift of perspective to help me was when my mum was in prison, I viewed her cell as a form of rehab to overcome her addiction and that her health will actually increase whilst being locked up. I instantly limited the sadness of the thoughts of my mum being in prison all through a shift in perspective.

The power of perspectives can be used to alleviate the pain of hardships and to turn something from negative to positive. I will give you two situations I have witnessed regarding how an individual's perspective can limit or even decrease their hardships.

Myself and my cell mate in HMP Wormwood Scrubs called Amjad, who had been charged with murder but not yet sentenced, had a discussion of how he's going to get through the potential numerous years he will be spending in prison and he told me:

"Although I'm locked up and it doesn't feel good, at least I have no distractions and I can wholeheartedly devote my life to God." He said if he was free he would likely be praying less, so his faith in god and his perspective of how he can now repent and become closer to god than ever before will alleviate the pain of being locked away.

I had another cell mate when I got transferred to another prison, which was HMP Highdown, and my cousin Richard had been in this prison for many years prior.

When I got to Highdown a week later, I was moved to the same cell block as my cousin, which was good as even though we were in the worst of places in life, we had spent good time together.

He had a friend he knew I'd get along with and that was my only cell mate during my time there called Akeel.

Akeel is very godly and spiritual and his perspective on his sentence was that god allowed this hardship to happen to save him from a more dangerous situation such as an early loss of life.

I believe it's important we grow through each experience we go through, but it's just as important to attempt to uphold a positive perspective on even the hardships we face, as this will absolutely decrease the pain.

You can alter your perspectives regarding things personal to you to not only limit or remove adversities, but to actually make you feel better regarding something that if not altered will continue to harm you.

Pay close attention to your perspectives, as it can do the opposite too. I see many people overlook their current blessings with a bad perspective which causes their suffering!

Ask yourself:

When rain falls from the clouds above does it only fall upon one house?

Stop being a victim with a bad perspective, rather radiate positivity even during adversity.

You can uphold positivity in negative scenarios, all as a consequence of a shift in perspective. All as a consequence of a shift in perspective.

You can use this to think positively about everything. For example, even if you feel misunderstood throughout your life, no longer feel bad about it or as if there is something wrong with you, rather view being misunderstood as you must be so uniquely special that it's a struggle for individuals to understand you and that's their issue.

Next time you're facing adversity, use this '**treadmill perspective**' to help you push on through and not let the adversity get the better of you.

Running on the treadmill, as we all commonly know, is both physically and mentally difficult, but by taking one step at a time forward through the adversity you will make progress in many ways. Your heart will beat healthier, your lungs will become more efficient at providing oxygen to your muscles, and your mind will be much clearer as exercise is a natural antidepressant towards stressing.

You will also increase your resistance because you'll be able to last longer with each run on the treadmill building up strength towards the adversity you've endured; so with adversity you've gained.

We should use this '**treadmill perspective**' to acknowledge that through difficulty we enhance our future selves.

As a believer of god, I also believe that god gives his hardest tests to those whom he knows has enough strength. Go through, and then grow through each experience. Without rain, the flowers wouldn't have such vibrant colours.

Using the power of perspectives to notice the good in the bad will make you a person full of much more happiness, positivity, and resilience.

After alleviating yourself of a negative perspective, you'll be elevated in both mental and physical health, for after evolving your perspectives, you will stop wasting time pondering on negative aspects of life.

This isn't about overlooking the pain, because the pain has to be endured to bring about the gain of the difficult experiences.

So it's about having a more positive outlook on life and realising the troubles of our past and difficulties of the future can actually be used to help, not hinder, our development.

Means of Motivation

There are many different means of motivation. Sometimes in life everything is going well and we have motivation in abundance, but at intervals we all know it gets difficult to maintain. I wanted to write this chapter to help people become more conscious of using all avenues to not just regain, but maintain motivation.

Using positive means of motivation, such as providing for and supporting family, ambition for wealth, wanting to be great at something, making a positive difference to your own life, freedom and most important of all- health; well these are the best ways to stay motivated and focussed. However, I want to express how we all can use our negative emotions and experiences to fuel the flame of motivation.

The negative means of motivation can be just as effective as the positive and I think as mental ill health cases are rising I want people to acknowledge that we can be motivated by the hardships we are facing or have already been through. With a change of perspective we can actually gain motivation from the happenings which normally sap us of our energy.

The negative fuel to motivate us can consist of:

•**Depression** is the ultimate motivator… hear me out, if you have suffered from depression before then you will most definitely never want to return to such a state of being. Therefore, this can motivate you to do anything and everything to achieve a stable and positive state of mind. Everything that once caused your depression can now be utilised to fuel your motivation for a better standard of life; turning sour to sweetness with your new perspective.

•**Feeling overwhelmed** by work can push you to do more work in a shorter period of time, meaning you will get things completed sooner. So the pressure of being overwhelmed can actually be the push you need to complete targets and tasks more efficiently.

•**Fear of failure** can help you maintain motivation because you do not want to fail at all costs and a person who never quits, never fails, for they keep on pushing through each obstacle. Only if you give up can you feel like you've been defeated, so a fear of failure can be a massive motivator. **Fear is a powerful motivator** because it makes us feel uneasy and we work hard to escape that feeling of discomfort. When utilised at intervals it can help us to push harder than ever before, but if fear is uncontrolled it will eventually become a burden and increase our stresses. Fear is the fire inside us which can light up our lives and make us shine brighter than ever, or if uncontrolled, can impact our will to act, burn our souls and defeat us of our strengths. **Dangers are real but fear is optional, choose to have courage over cowardice and faith over fear.**

•**Financial problems** with money at some stage of life, or even just thoughts of going without essential things in life can motivate an individual to work very hard to earn a better standard of life than experienced or envisioned.

•Negative thoughts can help you become a better version of yourself. I personally believe emotions such as shame, frustration, guilt, insecurity and other stresses we feel are there to show us a sign that aspects of our lives need improving. Think of it like a car's engine light showing us there is a problem. When we feel mental adversity, it's your brain telling you something could do with improving, changing or to remove aspects of your life completely. So let's gain motivation from the positives and negatives we feel, so we can then sail smoothly through the good and bad times, regardless of any obstacle, tide or wave we face in life. For we will gain good momentum with a perspective of *different means of motivation.*

The way fighters use fearing the worst outcome to fuel their preparation and push themselves to train harder than ever before, is exactly how we all should use our negative thoughts to benefit us instead of breaking us. We all get these thoughts at stages throughout our lives, so it's better to acknowledge how to utilise both positives and negatives to our favour.

When we hear of illness, let that help us strive to be healthier.

When thinking of death, let that help us live life to the fullest. Using both positive and negative means of motivation has been proven to help keep people maintaining productivity regardless of life's circumstances.

Increased understanding, increased resilience and elevated happiness, are all the consequence of a change of PERSPECTIVE.

9 AND 6 PERSPECTIVE

9 and 6. I want to use these numbers to express to you that from different places there are different truths, so when in an argument it is very possible that both parties could be right.

At first it seems rather odd that two individuals in conflict could be correct at the same time during their differences. Learning how to see from others' perspectives limits or cancels arguments even happening, for you will have greater understanding.

Now I want you to draw a number 9 in front of you…

From your point of view, the number remains 9, but to the person opposite you, that number is 6, and you'll both argue till the day's end that you're both individually correct.

Now by acknowledging the 9 and 6 perspective, next time you're in any form of disagreement try to see what the other person is seeing. This will increase your understanding and cancel out wasted energy and time arguing. This could help both business and personal relationships, so utilise the power of perspectives to increase your perception of situations.

There could be more than one perspective correct at the same time. As if the number 8 is in front of you, to you and the person opposite, the number remains 8, but to the individuals to the left and the right they both agree that it is the infinity sign. In life, always be open minded and remember that every single person's eyes has their own individual viewpoint. Each individual has their own set of pupils and no one can view exactly where you view from. As I mentioned that mental health is completely unique to a person, so are our perspectives and perceptions. Although we may share the same interests, morals and beliefs within our social circles, our realities are a result of what we uniquely perceive.

If you waved at someone through a window and they didn't wave back, it doesn't always mean they have blanked you. Their eyesight could've been blocked by the sun blazing on the glass. So stay open minded and before feeling negative emotions off the back of your perspective on situations, try to see from other perspectives for greater understanding before you let your feelings be affected. This will improve your standard of life, for if you verify a scenario before letting it affect you and opening up your mind to new ways of thinking this will lead you to have a massive increase in understanding.

Do not overthink people's actions too much because for every action there is a reason, as to the majority of madness there's a method. If you find yourself viewing life from a negative perspective then you and only you have to work towards altering your view on life. This is worth your effort for it will change the way you feel and perceive things.

Once we begin to understand the power perspectives have over our quality of life, we can then learn to gain from every pain and it will enhance our gratitude towards the good times. That's because we have more understanding of the good, the bad, and the in-between.

After reading the 9 and 6 perspective, you will be less likely to have fallouts with friends, family and co-workers. You will let go of grudges that you once held, for you realise that both individuals consider themselves correct from their perspective and perceptions. Here is to less arguing and less stress, all the result of deeper understanding and altered perspectives helping your quality of life. Your viewpoints need to be guided just like I mentioned in MENTAL PILOT. You're either the victim or the victor but it all begins with your viewpoint.

Which would you prefer?

Victim mentality or a resilient victor mentality?

The answer is clear, use your initial perspectives to set you off with the correct viewpoint to limit or remove negativity and make you feel more positive about aspects of life, whether good or bad in a better light.

Remember people see things from different places. A road sign telling you to go right will show left to the person opposite the sign, so don't expect everyone to agree with everything you agree with, because as we've established, we are all uniquely seeing life from our own personal perspectives. It's just like how we all have similar handprints and palms, but then under closer inspection we all have our own unique fingerprints.

Gratitude Perspective

Now that we are aware of how powerful perspectives truly are towards our current levels of happiness, we can alter our viewpoints to help us be happier. The same way I did so by simply noticing the good view outside the window instead of the iron prison bars, ensuring I remain captive in my cell, you can use altering your perspective to benefit you, as well. If I was focussed on the fact that I was locked in a concrete box then I wouldn't have been able to acknowledge the good that still surrounded me. Even in such circumstances, **both happiness and sadness is still a consequence of our own thoughts and perspectives**. You can help yourself by using the gratitude list to aid you to count your blessings instead of being plagued by stress. As we commonly know, energy flows where your focus goes, and I will also mention in the Consciousness chapter about how what we don't recognise is nonexistent to us. So whether that be overlooking our blessings or struggles, what we don't consciously notice is nonexistent to our minds, don't focus on what's lacking or problematic because then you're spending less time embracing what you're blessed to have. Most people don't realise what they have until after it is lost.

The gratitude list will have you appreciating all things before having to go without them. **There is always worse going on in the world and you shouldn't have to go through worse to appreciate where you now stand**. This isn't about just turning a blind eye to your problems or ignoring intrusive thoughts because as I mentioned I really do believe the thoughts that harm us are warning lights to help us improve. It's more about bringing forward all the small things we should have conscious gratitude for and about making us feel better for what we do have and not feeling worse off due to comparison to others.

Why would you want to go through another person's mind to see what you find?

Be yourself, appreciate that there is only one of you in the whole world and only you can be yourself. Don't compare yourself to anyone else. People often make the mistake of looking at others' situations and comparing and then wanting to have what they have or to be in their position. Now be careful about what you wish for because another person may have all of what you want but not have what you NEED. Why compare yourself to the lonely rich person who has no family or true friends when you have something in your life money can't buy?

Another reason comparison is very bad for your perspectives and can ruin your levels of gratitude is because there is always more than what meets the eye. A family from a community point of view could look like they're in perfect happiness and harmony, but in reality behind closed doors, the family has serious disagreements, fall outs and could be arguing daily. Allow this example to show you not to compare yourself to others through just visuals and keep in mind that people only show their good side in the public eye. Therefore you're comparing your mishaps and negatives to only the positives of others' lifestyles and it's very obvious after comparing your negatives to someone else's positives you're not going to feel uplifted are you?

Don't compare, instead love your life and by doing the gratitude list of 3, it will support you in doing just that.

Try this

Write out 3 things you are grateful for in front of you right now.

1-

2-

3-

You can use this gratitude list wherever you are, and upon doing this you will increase your awareness of more aspects of your own life to be grateful for. Again I say, if I could use this list inside a smelly HMP prison cell and improve my thoughts, feelings and emotions, then you as my reader can most definitely enhance your days with this list.

As I currently write this inside my cell, my gratitude list of 3 helps me feel better.

1- I'm grateful for a pillow upon which I can rest my head, no matter how uncomfortable this prison bed is, there are humans out there who are homeless and sleeping on cold concrete floors and in doorways of shops, so how can I not appreciate the hard blue mat I get to sleep on?

By me having this perspective of gratitude, it actually enhanced my quality of sleep each night, for I overcame complaining about the discomfort of these painfully broken bunk beds to then appreciating the situation of where I lay.

2- I'm grateful for the narrow view between the iron bars so I can get a small glimpse of nature passing by the prison walls, as some cell windows face brick walls, so I'm glad I get the view that I do.

My cellmate Akeel and I also get to feed the birds the leftover bread through the gaps of the window. There's honestly so many small things in this life that go unnoticed that we should all be grateful for. Once we acknowledge all these small aspects, our mood will improve massively, for we become aware of what we do have rather than what is lacking.

3- I'm grateful for the running water I have in my cell. People in other parts of the world have to walk miles upon miles to get what we easily take for granted and what we can just turn a tap for. I'm grateful for my Eritrean foster parents Kahsia and Ghidei who looked after me for 2 years in my early teens, teaching me about different types of difficulties people face in other parts of the world. Being aware of others who are less privileged helps me appreciate all the small blessings which are actually massive. If you have ever spent a day fasting you'll know how lucky we are to be able to eat and drink whenever we feel like it. Having daily nutrition is one of the many massive blessings that go unnoticed, so this gratitude list of 3 will help you become aware of all that is bestowed upon you. More time spent in gratitude and less time spent on focusing on the wrong things or giving energy to thoughts that ruin our days.

Remember:
You shouldn't have to lose something to appreciate its value!
Let's all be more grateful and notice all our blessings both big and small.

As I write this section I'm currently with my nephew Rayyan Sean who's had a 2 night sleep over with me and he's been drawing, playing video games and having fun whilst I'm writing and we're going to the museum straight after our breakfast and showers. Life is really nice in this current moment, I'm enjoying the present moment daily, only looking back to the past in times of reflection to see how far I have come or to analyse ways I can improve for the future, but living in this present moment wholeheartedly.

Looking back, if I could make myself happy in a prison cell then in the free world, using everything I mentioned in this chapter, you can and will most definitely improve your overall happiness. In desperate times of need, stay blessed by continuing to notice every small aspect of goodness instead of the bad.

Don't focus on what you don't have, don't be a victim of any experience, never focus only on what is lacking or problematic, because the emotions you will feel after viewing things from that perspective will not be pleasant.

Happiness does not come externally, to be full of love and joy we need to feel it internally first and then spread it out onto others.

The perspective of gratitude will cancel out many of your complaints due to deeper understanding. For example, how can a person complain in the warmth of their car about being stuck in traffic for 30 minutes when they know how it is through experience or are made aware of others walking in the rain to wait at a bus stop in the cold? Understanding different walks of life can instantly cancel out half of the complaints you have about your own.

Always be grateful for what you have. Being ambitious for more is great for pushing forward and making progress, but by being grateful for everything, this leads to a life of you never taking things for granted.

There are fellow humans out there who pray to be in the situation you are in.

What is **trash** to one, will be a **treasure** to another.

What one doesn't even notice they **have**, could be another's desperate **need**.

You don't have to go through poverty to appreciate not being poor, there is always more space in everyone's life for more gratitude.

Fasting from food is a great way to experience first hand what it is like to feel the pain of hunger and although you can break the fast whenever you feel like it, others in the world don't have the means and blessings to eat as soon as their hunger hits. Fasting helps increase your understanding of those less privileged and that's why in Islam, it is a duty for Muslims to help those less fortunate and after taking part in Ramadan, they increase their empathy to those suffering from hunger all around the globe.

It is important you acknowledge your blessings in life without losing them. This will lead you to much more daily happiness and the gratitude perspective list will ensure you are feeling uplifted.

You can use this list in all different places, whereupon completing this list in multiple places you will become more conscious of all the things you maybe once never noticed or took for granted. This results in an improved mood, all as the consequence of a change of perspective.

Everything you NEED is already in your life you just need to recognise this. Then you will stop seeking your best version externally. You have the power to obtain whatever it is you have wished upon, almost as if like magic. The reality is before anything came into physical existence, it was a thought inside someone's mind. From the invention of cutlery to assist us in eating, to the more mystical flying aluminium planes that seem to just float against gravity through the skies above us, and now rockets invented to go out into space, making even the sky not the limit. Keep a perspective that whatever it is you want, wish for, or need you can absolutely obtain. Don't let anyone else water down your sparks of inspiration, only you can be your best version and only you can envision the dreams you have for yourself. **Spend more time having faith in your dreams than seeking their validation!** Sometimes others' perspectives and life experiences can't even comprehend what it is you envision, so always keep faith in yourself, don't let your faith change due to someone else not seeing or believing in what you envision. **Could you imagine the multimillionaire YouTuber vloggers losing faith in their vision because when they said to their parents that they were going to do pranks and record funny videos for a living they were laughed at** and told to not be so stupid. Imagine they gave up their hopes and dreams?

Then they would've ended up working for someone else, potentially living a life of regret and sadness working a job they don't enjoy, all for not following through on what they envisioned for themselves. Always follow through on your dreams because dreaming doesn't cost you anything so why choose to dream cheap?

The reality is sometimes even your own parents can't see the path you can envision for yourself but don't limit your success because of others' life experiences and perspectives.

Do not seek validation from others when dream chasing, people can't feel what you're feeling or see exactly what you are envisioning. **Do you expect the doctor to feel the same pain his patient is explaining? No.** But that doesn't mean it's nonexistent, so keep faith in your own dreams and don't have a nightmare by letting others ruin who you want to be.

I want to mention someone who is extremely inspirational, **Matt Mac**, he is a blind recording artist and music producer from Garden Hill First Nation, Manitoba.

Born blind, he didn't have the best start to life, but that never stopped him from chasing his dreams. He found comfort in music and as I mentioned in **PASSION PURSUIT** it is of utmost importance to find healthy coping mechanisms in life. These can then become passions and purposes of ours. Through the comfort of music, he began writing songs and making beats, all whilst being blind he taught himself how to play piano and guitar.

Faith in yourself is the most important, you have the power every day to do things regardless of your circumstances. Have faith and don't seek validation. Massive respect and love to **Matt Mac,** he can't see but lacks no faith in his dreams, a true inspiration and even after being born with no eyes, his mindset assisted him to live a good life. He hopes to continue to use his platform to inspire others and he is doing just that. He wants people to acknowledge that they can achieve whatever they set their mind to.

Maintain faith in yourself at all times, do not exert energy seeking validation of your dreams, rather spend more time believing in yourself and maintain a positive perspective on life. It's of lofty importance to ensure your perspectives are upheld in a positive light, because if not altered or guided, the power of perspectives can work against you. You will end up seeing positive things in a negative way, you will end up overseeing the good you have and noticing all the bad instead. Don't become a victim to the power you can control. Be the victor not the victim by controlling your perspective on life and upholding a positive outlook.

So we've now established the true power of perspectives, we are aware of how crucial our viewpoints are towards our standards of life and how without altering our perspectives, it can be ruinous to our levels of understanding and happiness. You will most definitely enhance your well being by actively keeping your mind viewing the positive aspects of life. The positives we can obtain through our pain instead of only noticing what's lacking or problematic.

The planet we are living on has so much beauty for us to see, we just need to increase our consciousness towards what usually goes unnoticed.

When looking at life through *the treadmill perspective,* we can go through the difficulty knowing we will gain improvement.

When looking at life through *the 9 and 6 perspective,* we deepen our levels of understanding, limiting fall outs, all the whilst increasing our awareness towards others.

When looking at life through *the gratitude perspective,* even when we have less than others we will feel uplifted, for we are still grateful for what we have personally. We will be uplifted by things we once took for granted and even just a glass of water from the tap you will appreciate more, for you know there are others in the world who have no water.

When looking at life through *the trouble to triumph perspective* you will spend more time embracing the growth than enduring the suffering of each upsetting or adverse scenario. You will never self diagnose anything that is of disservice to yourself. When life happens it will never get the better of you, for each hardship you face you gain an enhancement.

As I write this, the sun is sitting upon a beautiful ocean blue sky, the trees are full of colour, leaves blowing in the warm summer breeze and birds are flying by as if to show us what it looks like to be free. Even in such circumstances of being locked in my cell, my perspective has me massively uplifted. At this very moment I was shocked at how I could control my thoughts, feelings and emotions by keeping a positive perspective in such negative circumstances.

Utilising the power of perspectives you can literally enhance your consciousness to all the good things you may have never even noticed before. How can a prison bed become more comfortable?

By considering how rough the homeless sleep.

Perspectives can make bad things feel a little better, but if not guided, can also make good things worse; such as those who always compare themselves to others. They'll never have enough, for they always want more in order to outdo the next person.

Install more understanding, gratitude, resilience and happiness to your life by increasing your consciousness with positive perspectives.

Artwork by Isabella P.

10
CONSCIOUSNESS

What you are aware of creates your reality, reality doesn't create what you are aware of.

What I mean by this is what we are conscious of becomes our realities.

Have you ever wondered how Earth can be the best place for some, a reflection of heaven, but for others Earth couldn't be worse, it's a reflection of Hell. This is all due to what each individual is aware of, leading to their realities reflecting their awareness.

So what you are conscious of becomes your reality. Consciousness creates reality so by learning and experiencing new things, we can improve our realities.

Before you became aware of something in life, it didn't exist to you.

This applies to many things. Before we experience different feelings, thoughts, sensations and environments, it's impossible to be entirely conscious of them. We can try to imagine such things but only through our experience, can we truly understand and become aware of them and as a result increase our consciousness.

How can you know of the love a parent has for their child before having kids?

You can observe and notice the unconditional love parents have for their children but only through having children yourself can you fully understand the depths of that type of love.

What you are conscious of becomes your reality but there is so much more in this life to learn and become aware of, that even if we lived a thousand lifetimes, we still wouldn't be able to experience and acknowledge everything, let alone with just one life. Now that we've established this, **it is fact that you can change your reality by handpicking knowledge to enhance your consciousness**. This will instantly improve your reality for the better. I think it is good we don't have enough time to become aware of everything, it means we can make use of our time to tunnel vision our focus to only target acknowledging the positive aspects of life. In order to create a more positive reality in return. The sooner we do so, the better.

It sounds like common sense, but it isn't so common for those stuck in pessimistic and negative ways. **Why spend the majority of your life in sadness when it is a consequence of being conscious of only the bad and negative aspects of life?**

Start to study miracles and success stories, as this will increase your daily positivity and you will be more willing to try new things. You will become aware of good outcomes which will result in willingness to try new things. Instead of obliviously consuming negativity, this is why I personally don't watch the news very often, it's not because I'm burying my head in the sand from the world's troubles like the myth of the ostrich, it is because during lockdown I watched the news daily and it resulted in even my dream state being affected, I had weird vivid dreams of war breaking out with

China. I also had dreams that covid was an apocalypse and not to mention the daily sad stories the news covers. The news affected me daily in a negative way so I had to stop myself from watching it. Run a trial of any news channel right now and calculate how many stories are negative and how many are positive. You'll soon realise the percentages are highly negative and how we blindly add negativity to our conscious and subconscious minds, resulting in our reality becoming negative as well. Instead of obliviously adding negativity, purposefully choose what you give focus to, **have curiosity towards positivity,** choose positive stories to read. These could be success stories, more knowledge of aspects that will enhance your lives personally, there is no one size fits all. Learn about anything you feel will enhance your consciousness for the better. I will suggest one program for you all to watch, which will increase your consciousness of the power and beauty of this planet in which we all reside, which is:

ONE STRANGE ROCK by *National Geographic* produced by Darren Aronofsky.

Recognise

It is pivotal towards your development that you actively choose to become aware of and recognise more good aspects of life. **The more insight you have, the more you will have in sight.** With knowledge you recognise more, and as your consciousness expands your reality expands as well. There are so many positive aspects in our lives that we often overlook because we are preoccupied with problems surrounding negativity. We need to try to look beyond the negatives, then expel the constant thoughts of failures and sorrows from our consciousness. In doing so we will prevent being pessimistic people.

What we are conscious of will also impact our perspectives. I will give you an example...

There was a couple spending the day in the park because the weather was nice and they were having a good time whilst enjoying the sun. Then many hours passed and the sun moved across the sky. Now the sun was in its hottest hour and there was a tall oak tree that was in the way of a section of sunlight...
The man got annoyed by this and said the tree was blocking the sunlight and was frustrated by the position of the tree.
Then the woman politely pointed out to her partner that the tree isn't blocking the sunlight, but rather it is providing shade to those who want to be cool during this hour...
The lady was conscious of the positives of the tree being in the way of the sun and the man wasn't. We must become more conscious of the good that everything provides instead of solely noticing the negatives.
Only the aspects of life we recognise and acknowledge will be of bother to us...
This isn't about being ignorant to problems or situations but it is to state that what we recognise will truly determine the things that bother us. What we fail to recognise doesn't mentally affect us.
This is how people say that being ignorant is to be blissful because the ignorant person will be lacking the awareness of problems and overseeing negativity in the process, meaning the lack of awareness results in ignorant individuals not noticing problems or negative occurrences.
After we know of something, that's when its impacts arrive, we need to always maintain a curiosity towards positivity. I'll further express how what we don't recognize won't bother us:
Let's say you have a friend who has arachnophobia, which is an intense fear of spiders.

If they don't consciously recognise that there is a spider very close to their pillow and they haven't yet seen it, will it affect them or cause them stress?

What you don't recognise becomes nonexistent. Attempt to always overlook negative things and pay them no attention, as the moment you allow yourself to recognise and be amongst negativity is the moment you're downloading negative things into your consciousness.

Another event which further expresses that what we aren't aware of doesn't bother us is when you didn't know a person who you considered a friend was backbiting you and speaking badly about you. This individual could've said all these bad things months upon months ago but only when you become aware of it does it trigger your emotions.

You must keep a close eye on those around you because if you continue to communicate with those who are negatively conscious then you will ingest their negative thoughts and feelings. You will also become negatively conscious.

It isn't bad at all to remove people who drain your energy and it is wise to analyse which friends are constantly complaining because these friends will have an affect on how you're internally feeling. We need to try to notice and remove negativity or we need to decide to avoid even recognising anything that will dampen our emotions and feelings.

Your nose is in front of your eyes right now but you look straight past it to focus on this page. You don't consciously notice it, let this example show you that we can look past negative situations in the process of seeking positivity.

You didn't recognise your nose in your viewpoint until you thought about it, so let's think more positively and notice the blessings in front of our eyes. Refer back to the gratitude perspective to help assist you on being conscious of all the things you should be grateful for.

The moment you recognise and become aware of something is the exact moment it causes you to have emotions. This applies to everything in life, both positive and negative. The aspects of life that you want to stop from bothering you; consciously decide to attempt to give it no recognition for a while and see how you feel after doing so. **Doing this will limit its impact upon you.** Try to overlook negativity and continually add positivity as this will shift your perception of life into a more positive place.

Self Study

It is equally important to study and become aware of new aspects of life to improve your consciousness.

Why? Why is that just as important? Because your knowledge and awareness of life creates your reality, the more positive experiences and knowledge you gain, will result in a more positive reality and version of yourself.

This is exactly why I suggest reading as much as you possibly can because you learn and become aware of many studies and receive advice from people from all walks of life. Remember I stated we don't have enough time to learn everything… we must utilise our time wisely and study all of that which enhances us personally. I have a question, how often has the academic knowledge you gained in school been of use to you in adult life?

Many people coming from where I come from consider studying to consist of only topics from the high school classroom. This couldn't be further from the truth, through self study you can learn about anything you want to, with no teacher standing over you and no set topics to choose from, you can literally enhance your knowledge on any study you want. **Don't ever say you don't enjoy studying, you just haven't studied something you enjoy yet.** When you realise through self study you can improve yourself with no physical limit, you may well turn from a gym freak as I was to a book head doing reps of pages. Your physical muscles have limits to their growths but your consciousness has no limit at all, for as I mentioned, a thousand lifetimes wouldn't be enough to experience all this planet has to offer. With the chapter **Passion Pursuit**, regarding locating new passions that align with you, you can also apply to self studying. Study what's authentically you, **study isn't boring and when you find topics you enjoy studying, you will never have another day of boredom.**

I personally have found that there are so many extremely fascinating things to learn about on this planet. Anything you find interesting you can begin to study further. I get captivated by the fascination of the solar system and science to the point I could spend hours reading about it, which is much better than spending hours overthinking or being bored doing next to nothing.

Invest time into learning, as I mentioned in Passion Pursuit your passions will be of aid to you, as well as entertain, all while increasing your knowledge, which is a complete win-win.

Now that you have begun to work on your consciousness, don't beat yourself up if you find yourself feeling negative or if you occasionally revert to bad habits which you intended to stop. Rather be grateful that you are self aware and you have begun to work on self development, because there was a time when you were ignorant.

Analyse the content you watch daily and the accounts you follow on social media because the post you see with your eyes will be posted into your mind.

If we want to improve the things we are conscious of, with all the hours we spend on our electronics, **it is more important than ever to choose wisely what is on our screens.**

What you are conscious of is what will bother you; have you ever been consciously reminded of train bombings whilst on the tube? If so then you will know how affected we are by what is brought to our attention and how what you are conscious of will instantly affect your thoughts, feelings, and emotions. This is exactly why I continually learn of positive stories and aspects of life to help me become more positively conscious.

I will talk more in the part 2 sequel of this book about how what we imagine or learn, impacts our will towards taking action in life. Still, we also need to be cautious regarding what we learn because it will change the way we perceive reality. Our subconscious mind doesn't differentiate between what is real and what is fake, we need to be cautious about the information we ingest, for it will soak into our subconscious minds, and could literally turn false and harmful rumours into what you believe and can result in an individual losing touch with reality.

For example:

Millions of parents worldwide for the first 10 years of their children's lives, create an atmosphere for their children to believe that Santa Claus is real. Now if you ask a 7 year old if Santa Claus is real, that 7 year old will promise you with their hand on their heart that he is because they've seen handwritten letters left by Santa himself, to half eaten cookies and naughty elves causing mischief around the house in the month of December. So what I want us to establish from this is, the content and information we allow to surround us or allow ourselves to see and read daily, will impact the way we perceive reality to be. I also want every reader to contemplate that if we as humans for 10 years can believe in something that isn't even real, then **we can most definitely believe in ourselves.**

If the actions of those around us can have us as children believing in Santa, then if we limit our knowledge and never try to seek out more information as adults, we will continue to believe in false prophecies.

We need to take the first steps in being our own heroes and it begins with adding and ingesting positive information into our consciousness. This results in our lives becoming more positive. I know I have repetitively said this same thing, but I really hope you put this to practise because **I've used this after many dark happenings in life to quickly brighten my darkest of times.** After some hardships I can't mention, I was in such a dark place that I didn't even notice that the flowers had colours. I was beginning to go down the wrong path, becoming more conscious of seriously dangerous things, which would have resulted in one of two things: early death or a long spell in prison. As I always say, **I only preach what I have practised.**

I know from experience that when applying daily information of better circumstances, you can change your whole reality into whatever it is you want your reality to be. Every single creation on this planet was a thought before it existed, even the words within this book were once just a thought of a potential idea. It is only with active effort that we will make a true difference regarding what we are conscious of. Reality will move in the direction of our consciousness.

We have deep rooted stereotypes that just aren't true, so we need to work towards breaking down such stereotypes and moving forward towards **a life of unity with those in our communities.**

Although some statistics can be shown to give guidelines to the likelihood of where danger may arise, we can't allow these stereotypes to let us judge people by their place, appearances, race or culture.

We need to be aware that there is good and bad in every walk of life, Yin with Yang and Yang with Yin. We need to be open minded and willing to learn new things. There is no limit or age that can stop us from increasing our consciousness; there are so many similarities within all religions and cultures. Do not allow us humans to be broken up into sections. Look at how every belief holds family in high importance, how every belief is to enhance yourself to become a better person, how whether it is meditation or prayer, we practise ways to praise our creator.

I have Irish, English, Eritrean and Afghan family members, I have friends from Jamaica, Uzbekistan, Somalia, America, Yemen, Canada, Philippines and I was locked in a cell with Amjad who is from Pakistan for 23 hours a day in a space not much bigger than a bathroom and then spent 4 months in a cell with Barlow who is from Guyana.

All cultures and all people from all different places have so much knowledge of their own to share with each other. We need each other, whether it be to teach one another better ways of meditating, better tasting food or smarter ways of living, we all should embrace one another. Although some have different beliefs, some drink alcohol until they can't walk straight, some pray 5 times a day, some fast as a sacrifice to god, some are non-holy but have good hearts. Be conscious of the good in each and every one of us, as no one is perfect and it's perfect not to be perfect.

Don't be close-minded and live in ways where you limit the chance to experience or live amongst different cultures or races of people. I can assure you we can learn at least one thing from absolutely anyone.

Do not blame your upbringing for being an individual that is close minded because it is our responsibility to self study and increase our own knowledge of life. If we all had followed in the exact same footsteps as those before us how would humanity have ever made progress?

Remember your beliefs will mirror the information you ingest. For example:

If you only ever studied that Pitbull dogs are violent, have locked jaws, and attempt to bite anyone that gets too close, then anytime you see a Pitbull you will instantly fear them. However, in reality I have a Pitbull and he's 2 years old now and he doesn't even bite back the small dogs when they bite him, and he runs away from my 5 year old nephew Rayyan when Ray chases him. **So don't believe all you hear and only trust half of what you see.** Actively strive towards doing your own research to grow your consciousness in the right direction, which will lead you to become more open-minded and understanding. After doing so you will perceive reality from a more favourable viewpoint, you will knock back the fears and anxieties which may have once had power over you, and you will become a person who is in possession of increased knowledge, awareness, and understanding.

You will become someone who is overall better to be around, but *for me what is better than improving myself is the power to uplift others and impact my loved ones in a positive way*. Even whilst in prison I never once put my burden onto others, although I'm sure they missed me as much as I missed them. I always try my best to not put my problems onto others but instead be there for my loved ones whenever needed.

I only want to discuss solutions to problems instead of constantly discussing the issues. I aim to have more knowledge of the solutions for life's daily problems instead of being solely conscious of all the troubles.

Although adrenaline can push and pull us through times of turmoil, it is much wiser to increase your knowledge of solutions to the problems before having to endure more adversity. Do you ever wonder how the humans who have lost what no money could ever compensate but still remain somewhat positive even through such hardships?

They do so by increasing their consciousness towards what they do have control over and making the most of any of the circumstances they have faced. Never feel like you're the only one suffering from the ways you're feeling and thinking. We are all human beings and as a human you will feel all emotions life has to offer at different intervals. The highs, the lows and all the in-betweens.

You are not alone, remember when it is raining and you're getting wet, you ain't the only one the clouds are raining on. They're raining on other humans, plants and animals too. Never feel like the weather is bad just for you and remember that those negative thoughts can be used to benefit you, but it's up to you how you react to them.

You have the power to choose to do the healthiest thing that calms your thoughts and makes you happy. Do everything that keeps your consciousness in a positive place. Many people in difficulty turn to the wrong coping mechanisms and that will become a downward spiral.

Maintaining your mindset is progressional because at least it isn't declining. When enduring agonies you may have lost some battles but you have survived and that is a victory in itself. Don't be hard on yourself, be self-loving, and after experiencing agonies you will feel more ecstasy the next time you face better circumstances as you would've empirically felt the difference.

To find inner happiness you need to stop seeking it from external things. You will grow into an internally more happy person. If you don't pay attention to what you add to your consciousness then brace yourself for more negativity causing you turbulence. You can't expect to become positive without actively learning and surrounding yourself with negativity. This applies to you also having to remove those who are constantly negative, who like to put their sorrows on your shoulders continuously. You will need to evade spending time with those who are so negatively conscious. It is your responsibility as an adult to transition from your past experiences and with intent become a positive person.

Responsibility

One way to get organised and make progress is simply to mind your own business. We need to focus on improving ourselves and take full responsibility to do so.

As adults we need to accept that we are responsible for the role of improving our awareness. Many negative things can happen that impact us and remain on our minds for a long time, but it is our own responsibility to add positive knowledge to help assist us through as well as beyond past and future difficulties. With increased knowledge you will also gain new opportunities. **There is no limit to what you can achieve**, but you first need to be responsible with what you allow your brain to consume. Those who eat healthily count their daily calories. Pay close attention to all the food you eat. It is just as important to pick positive information for our brains to examine as our consciousness will process what we experience or study regardless if it's healthy for us. You will increase your strengths by adding knowledge to your consciousness. For example, learning that Coca Cola had serious struggles in the first few years of business trade, this may be the information you need to assist you in becoming more resilient towards thoughts of quitting after initial difficulty in a new business. Knowledge is power, it isn't just a fancy saying, it will strengthen you towards any happenings. Equipped with more understanding you will have more resilience. With more insight you will recognise more and could also give advice to your friends and family wherever needed. Knowledge will lift you up and beyond many hardships due to possessing more understanding.

One of the most important powers of knowledge is that it cancels out <u>overthinking.</u> When you understand a situation you don't need to be overthinking about it. You won't exert so much energy in the process, overthinking harms millions throughout different stages of their lives. Don't let the what ifs be catastrophic and with more knowledge you will spend less time overthinking and more time in understanding and/or learning of solutions to any problem. A wise person finds solutions for problems. A person lacking knowledge will think first about the problem in everything. Do not be pessimistic in life and always try to gain insight to assist you. Any wise person knows that they know nothing at all. As I said, with 1000 lives we couldn't even come close to learning everything. Choose what information will be best for you to ingest and then grow into your smartest version.

YOU are responsible for improving your consciousness daily.

As children we never had the power to control all the things we saw, our parents made the decisions for us, but that doesn't stop infants from being curious. Regain your curiosity, but this time aimed at only positivity.

When a video game or movie has a minimum age requirement, why do you think that is?

It is because you can't place violence or content of discretionary viewing into the minds of children before they have become entirely conscious of right and wrong.

Knowledge is powerful, those adults who have had a seriously troubled childhood that resulted in their adult lives being involved in crime or plagued by mental adversities often get lower sentencing from the judges. Why's that? Because the individual wasn't guided to a healthy conscience and didn't seek conscious improvement. These individuals require more help than others. Local resources have an abundance of help available to those suffering with mental illness inflictions. I hope to help as many as possible because it is highly likely that the individual undertakes certain actions due to a very limited consciousness. It's possible they have heightened awareness of the wrong things.

As adults we need to **take responsibility** for what we give our energy to because we have more control over every aspect of our lives. So by accepting that our realities are a creation of our own doing, whether on purpose or obliviously, we can then begin to hold ourselves accountable for the reality we've created. If we feed into negativity and then we feel negatively impacted, it is our own fault. Don't feed your demons the energy they require to exist and they will soon disappear. Do more of what conquers your negative thoughts. Even if the action only conquers those negative thoughts for a single day, then that action needs to be a DAILY DOING. As I do with fitness, it's as if my negative thoughts sweat out of my body with every drop of perspiration.

We aren't always responsible for the ways we are feeling but we are responsible for remaining close to the aspects of life that are harming us. Never sacrifice your own mental stability for anything, love can quickly turn to hate when an individual sacrifices themselves to no prevail. Love is a beautiful feeling and of course most good things worth having don't come with ease and in some scenarios love grows even stronger through hardship, but this only happens when the hardships are external. Love should be easy going and calm our stresses, *quieting our bad thoughts, not creating them*, and instilling strength within.

We are responsible for the way things affect us continuously because we all have the human power of free will to remove ourselves from troublesome scenarios. I'll give you an example: I could spend my days disputing the sentence the judge gave me, saying I shouldn't go to prison, but I need to accept responsibility. I'd rather that situation didn't happen but in all honesty, so many blessings were bestowed upon me through that sentence. I got to spend good time with my cousin Richard. I read 120 books within that time and I met some good hearted people in the darkness of prison. You want to know how I transformed myself from an anger infused person who came from a troubled childhood? Simply by increasing my consciousness towards a better way of living, and although the scars of the past still remain on my soul and some on my skin, I've done a good job on feeling then healing all of them. The flashbacks of my dad's body, cold and grey, doesn't harm me in a bad way anymore for it makes me cherish the days we do have here on this beautiful planet. As a believer of god, I consciously don't fear death due to my beliefs of the afterlife. That means getting to see my family and friends again who have already passed away.

Some days I may appear aggressive and unapproachable but it's because I've laid one too many roses on coffin boxes and some days I need to just enjoy my own spiritual seclusion. I am far from perfect but I have a purpose of wanting to help others. I want you to contemplate right now that if I can do it, someone who has lived without parental advice since 9 years old, someone who has had to earn everything they have ever owned, someone who has had to pull himself back from the deepest depths of darkness in times of lacking hope. You can most definitely move towards living the life you have always wanted and move yourself towards a more positive and well-suited direction for the future.

As you are improving,
And you are improving,
You'll begin to notice.

The most effective way to improve your life positively is to add bits and pieces of positivity all across your day in every way. If your bank (mind) account is on minus (negative) there is only one way to change this… add currency (positivity) to not just get even, but you want to be wealthy in currency (positivity). Continue to work towards increasing your consciousness of better outcomes and you will perceive reality in such a heavenly way.

Many people read books of self help but fail to put the advice into practice. This isn't about you just having something to read as entertainment; all the minutes, hours, days, weeks and months I spent writing this was for the purpose of helping those who read it to make positive changes. For a long time I have been giving verbal advice to my friends, but with this book I'm hoping to reach and help those that I wouldn't have been able to otherwise. The contents of this book can hopefully help people improve their daily lives because it helped me. **I only preach about things that I have practised.**

If you ever feel like life is getting too much for you, spontaneously do something you never do. It could be a good laugh or you could regret it and want to return back to being you. This is the best tactic to make an impact, even with writing, I'll spend 4 six hour days writing at home and then change location. Spontaneously going somewhere I've never been to write and then it could result in me just having a refreshed feeling or it could be so noisy that I can't focus and I look forward to returning back to my usual location. Every small piece of a puzzle creates the picture, all things matter, learn to enjoy all forms of weather for they all play a crucial purpose. You are responsible for adding more positive pieces to your conscious puzzle. Some good people enter our lives and increase our positivity, but the responsibility is always on you to enhance yourself into a better version and create a better quality of life.

Observe Your Thoughts

What you are conscious of impacts everything in your life but in this section I will focus on how our thoughts need to be analysed before we allow these thoughts to impact our lives. You are the awareness behind your thoughts. The thoughts can't control you if you observe them and analyse the reason why you're thinking of such things. The moment you realise you are separate from your thoughts, is the moment you detach from their instant impacts. If we were our thoughts I think there wouldn't be a single human on this planet who hasn't spent time in prison. We don't get judged for our thoughts, we get judged for our actions.

Observe yourself, observe your thoughts, and then observe the situation surrounding you and what is making you think the way you're thinking.

It is pivotal that we become aware of the fact we are the consciousness behind our thoughts and although we aren't entirely separate from how we think, we are the being who can decide on which thoughts to pay attention to and which thoughts we shouldn't. This is why it's important to begin triple observation of your thoughts.

We need to analyse our thoughts because as we get older our imaginations become our enemy. This happens to millions of people, leading to an increase in cases of anxiety but individuals who have kept their imaginations of benefit are the people who don't see limits to what they can achieve. These people who pioneer completely new pathways and careers of which no one could've envisioned for them. I will have more content in part 2 of this book regarding impacts of our imaginations.

We are the human being behind the thinking, we are the consciousness behind the thoughts. We are not our thoughts; everyone at some stage will experience negative thoughts that harm them, does that mean they're self harming? Of course it doesn't. We do not choose the thoughts we think. This is because we are the conscious being behind the thought, but **YOU** most definitely need to begin to OBSERVE YOUR THOUGHTS. Observing your thoughts and taking a step back from constantly being affected with the thoughts you are receiving, you will be increasing your understanding of why and how you feel certain ways at times. Use mental pilot as a guide to analyse when and why you get negative thoughts and what to do to limit or remove them.

Become aware of the potential causes of your thoughts becoming negative. As I said with the news, I opted to take active effort into avoiding it. I observed my thoughts and whereupon doing so I soon realised that the news was causing a large percentage of my negative thinking.

We are not thoughts, we are humans, we can't always control the thoughts we get but we can observe our thoughts and observe where our thoughts help us and where our thoughts are of detriment to us.

You can't charge a man for having thoughts of killing, he hasn't taken action, he is just as innocent as the man who didn't get a thought to kill. You may have to be wary of him but you can't charge him for having those thoughts because just like when we have sad thoughts, did we decide to have them?

Do we ever decide to overthink to the point it hurts our emotions and feelings?

Do we decide to overthink at times when we need to focus or we are trying to sleep? No.

Did those who sadly passed away decide to have suicide on their minds?

No!

This is why it's of top importance to always observe your thoughts and try to understand why we fall into certain ways of thinking. Thoughts are not negative, thoughts are needed for our very existence. Every invention begins with a single flash of thought. In the chapter Fast Forgotten Thoughts, which will be in the part two version of this book, I will shed more light on the importance of writing down inspirational thoughts.

The same way inspirational thoughts can change our lives for the better, is the same way intrusive thoughts can harm us and affect our lives for the worse.

We need to analyse all of our thoughts and remember which decisions we made that led to increased positive thoughts and which decisions led us to thinking negatively.

Observing thoughts is a really good way to increase your consciousness because as with my analogy about the mind bank and having to add currency to get out of minus, this is exactly how observing our thoughts can assist us by increasing our awareness of when and why our thoughts turn negative. This helps us to avoid feeling such a way.

This will help prevent thoughts from being of detriment to our consciousness. It doesn't take a genius to know that the thoughts we get doesn't always reflect our realities, but if left unattended these non reality thoughts will soon change the way you perceive things. When being observant you will always notice when the quality of your thoughts is declining, when you need to listen closely to the ways you're feeling, or when you need some time out for yourself to be spiritually secluded.

If we don't maintain our consciousness and mental stability then we can't be the person we want to be. We can't uphold being the person who uplifts others, so make sure you listen and observe your inner self.

Make sure you maintain your well-being first so that you will be capable of doing well for others.

Enjoy the mystery of life and live everyday as if it is your last. **Do not** spend too much time stuck in thought about the things which hinder your happiness.

Many people stress about the uncertainty of the future but if they knew everything that was going to happen they would be even more stressed. Imagine if you knew the exact happenings of the future.

All the good and bad things that are due to happen, that will cause more stress than just embracing the unknown. Don't allow the uncertainty of the future to bother you because if you knew it all, it may well cause you more turbulence than peace.

I used to have a bad outlook on counselling, not due to experience, but because I used to think how could a counsellor advise me through something they haven't gone through themselves? Back then I was unaware of how counsellors are trained to be able to analyse an individual's thoughts and provide them with positive means to cope. Many of these coping mechanisms can help alleviate several forms of mental suffering. **Do not allow your thoughts to be negative in regard to something you haven't yet tried or experienced** because your thoughts could be limiting your self development.

What do you do when your mind is full of sadness, anger, anxiety, envy or any other negative thoughts or emotions? You should first observe why you feel such a way and why you're thinking the way you're thinking, as this will help you understand why you feel as you do, then remind yourself that we are not our thoughts, we are the being behind the thinking and if we all were our thoughts I think planet Earth would be a complete prison.

There isn't anyone who is completely free from negative thinking, however it is our responsibility to attempt to improve our ways of thinking and feeling.

You do have the strength to do that.

When feeling fear, be courageous and have faith.

When feeling anxious, calm your imagination and mind; be present.

If you feel hate because someone has done you wrong you can cancel it with gratitude that you have been exposed to the individual's real character.

When angry, remember that one act in anger can lead to a life full of regret.

The importance of observing your thoughts can't be understated as you increase more self awareness. You will become more conscious of what is good for you and what is of detriment; which will make life more enjoyable and easier after you understand yourself better.

We are our own Consciousness Creators.

Our Consciousness Creates Our Reality

If you have lived through many hardships, just like myself, then you can use this concept to help you.

I want you to imagine the scales of justice...

In this concept we will call it the scales of positive and negative. One side positive, one side negative, with us between the two. In my concept we ain't targeting a balance between both, we want to get so far positive that even when something bad happens we learn to maintain the power of a positive perspective.

If you are enduring hardships, struggling from past experiences, or even just find yourself feeling down as we all do at times, then your scales ain't doing you any justice because they're leaning towards negative.

Add more positivity to your consciousness to regain balance and then continue to be positive to maintain yourself feeling happy. I feel like the negative thoughts we feel and hear at times are there to help not hinder us. They're warning signals that something needs changing and when reacting to them with improving ourselves we will grow through each and every experience.

The scales of positive and negative can at any time be thrown in any direction because many things happen in life completely out of our control, but what is in our control is that we are the consciousness behind our beings and we have the responsibility to maintain the positivity of the scales. We need to try our best to at least maintain but we should all be aiming for scales that are heavily one sided, positively.

The content of this chapter will help you do just this, put it into practice and seek more constructive knowledge. Upon doing so you can land yourself in a powerful position of conscious positivity, so that even when something negative occurs, you are able to see the positives. This will make you overall so much happier, to be able to oversee opposing circumstances and instead view the potential gains from each negative occurrence. You become undefeated. You will transform troubles to triumphs.

Sadly but surely with this powerful position of conscious positivity, there exists its opposite, a really detrimental position of conscious negativity.

These people are very pessimistic, true residents of evil, they become so negative that they find negativity in positive things and give so much more time to complaining about problems and no time at all to being grateful of their blessings and fail to instal faith into potential solutions.

These people feel genuine hate for those doing better than them and envy is second nature to them. Gratitude is regarded by them as accepting to have less. Instead of them embracing gratitude as simply and importantly appreciating everything. They complain even when good things happen, for they compare to others, they never enjoy the present moment.

They are negative daily and read articles regarding all sorts of negative things, reposting negative things on social media to spread that sad information onto others.

These are anchor people, who will try to hold you back when you're trying to set sail and move forward.

The scales of positive and negative can help individuals suffering from negative awareness to build themselves back towards their best, and begin to live life more positively again.

The scales can also help already positive individuals maintain being positive and to gain insight of the negatives of which to avoid, for example:

Studying the mistakes of the generation before you can save you from making mistakes and ending up in mental turmoil due to unhealthy coping mechanisms. Learn of the errors of those before us, by learning of the impact heavy alcohol consumption or drug use had on individuals, both psychological and physically. It will help maintain their positive position in life by avoiding adding negatives to their scales of justice. Many people, when times are going well, take drugs on weekends or just at times of celebration but most definitely don't count yourself immune to the impact of substance abuse, because my mother has a true heart of gold and I know for a fact she loves her children and even having a young princess daughter younger than the age of 6 couldn't stop her feeling the urge of addiction.

SO DON'T EXPERIMENT

You think you have the strength to avoid addiction?
Say that to a mother who has lost her children!

Don't make the mistakes that those before us have made, keep your mind, soul and body in a healthy state. Focus daily on adding all different means of positivity to your consciousness.

Now that you have read this, you have gained the concept of the scales of positive and negative to help your existence and assist you in living a better quality of life. Be purposefully curious of positivity and your reality will follow. Enjoy.

You will be a pragmatic, not problematic person after learning and putting this chapter to practise.

The brain is more like clay than cement, it can be changed and moulded at any moment but not instantly. You will need to be patient with the improvement of your consciousness and it will absolutely be worth every second you invest. An atheist can be a believer of god tomorrow and vice versa. Don't ever allow yourself to feel like you're stuck or limited to one way of living when life, just like our consciousness, is ever-changing.

Neurotransmitters in the brain can be repaired and rebalanced to help your brain function better and it is important to maintain the balance of the chemicals in the brain. These chemicals play a key role in the ways you feel, think, and function.

There is a therapy called '**Amino Acid Therapy**' which is used to normalise the chemicals in the brain that affect your personality and moods. Do further research about this form of therapy if you feel depressed at intervals to a cause that you can't figure out.

An imbalance of the chemicals in the brain has been linked to depression and diseases. Your neurotransmitters will malfunction without the balance of amino acids.

There are many benefits of taking amino acids.

They provide an energy source, help to build muscle, sustain a normal digestive system, maintain healthy hair, skin and nails, make hormones and neurotransmitters, and boost your overall immune system.

The perception of life you have isn't entirely of your own doing because we grow through experience that weren't of our creation. You need to acknowledge that you do have the power to gradually shift your perception by learning of purposeful information to assist you in having a better outlook on life and becoming conscious of the aspects of life which make you feel better.

There is so much on this planet to experience and learn. Never feel stuck in negative ways.

Do new things to boost your life experiences and ingest information to increase your knowledge. With more experiences and knowledge you will have the wisdom needed to help others!

Empirically become your best version. Consciousness expands through experiences so don't be shy to try new things in life. Every person has their own unique awareness, their very own unique ways of thinking, feeling and their own perception.

It is very important what you allow yourself to become aware of. What we are conscious of impacts our will to take action. Being conscious of negativity could stop an individual from doing what they really want to do. Our consciousness impacts our lives massively. The man who wanted to swim in the sea but had so called 'human-eating sharks' on his conscious, refuses to dive overboard out of being conscious of the sharks. His imagination impacted his will to do what he wanted, when in reality there is a higher chance of the boat sinking than the man being eaten in a vast ocean full of nutrition for the so-called human-eating sharks. Movies implant serious false beliefs into our consciousness and impact our imaginations for the worse. After reading this chapter, pay close attention to what you study, read, watch and see for it will impact your reality.

If you want to improve, you will need to change your ways, we cannot remain the same and expect a different outcome or better sense of feeling. As we grow through these chapters, take notes and put these ideas to practise. They have all worked for me personally, I'm sure they could work for you in one way or another.

Yours truly,

Mr. Sean Atlas Walsh

A NOTE ABOUT THE AUTHOR
FROM THE EDITOR OF THIS BOOK

An author generally takes great pride in their ability to select the right words for every piece of writing they partake in. That is certainly the case for myself, and yet here I am struggling to choose which ones to use in order to describe Sean Atlas Walsh. The issue isn't anything to do with a lack of fitting words, but rather there are so many positive aspects about the author of *The Not So Common, Common Sense* that I'm having a difficult time being limited to a single page when telling you about him. I suppose the only solution is to use words which detail the qualities that have stood out the most to me about Sean in the time I have known him.

Warrior

Have you heard the legends of the gladiators who risked their lives and fought for glory in the Colosseum? The spirit of those champions lives on in Sean Walsh. He is a warrior at heart, a defender of his honour and the honour of those who are dear to him.

Friend

Friend is such a simple word to describe a relationship that has so much held within it. You don't call someone a friend unless they've got your back and have your best interest at heart. A friend is someone you can share a laugh with but also confide in about the most important aspects of your life. I can, without a doubt, tell you that the author of this book is an individual who anyone would be fortunate to call their friend.

Seeker

This is a title I don't hand out lightly, as I consider it one of the most dominant qualities in myself. A seeker is one who is searching to understand and experience the existential truths about this life, the world around them, and their relationship with the source of creation itself. Sean is a sincerely spiritual and godly human being. I admire his perspectives and open-mindedness about the mystical aspects of life.

***

I consider it a great privilege to have played a part in bringing this book to fruition. Since you've already finished the book at this point, it goes without saying that Sean is also a top-tier wordsmith. He expertly conveys advice and tactics that his readers can actually put to practice in their daily lives. I wish my 'brother across the pond' to have great success, happiness, and health in all that he goes on to do.

-   Mason J. Schneider

You can keep up with Sean via his Instagram @seanatlaswalsh

Acknowledgements

I am truly grateful to each and every person who has helped me at different intervals throughout this book-writing journey. No matter how big or small, each action of assistance has enabled me to bring this book into existence. There is truly no end to my gratitude.

I would like to thank myself for working hard each and every day, even on the days when I haven't felt my best!

I want to thank my editor who is an author in his own right, Mason J. Schneider, who has become a good friend of mine.

I want to thank the following individuals as well, friends who I consider my family, and that have played an integral part in my life and the creation of this book:

Tony T.

Isabella P.

Annalise B.

Romano L.

Sinead Walsh

Siobhan Walsh

Tom M.

Sanchez L.

Richard M.

Akeel B.

Ahmed A.

Mohammed H.

Gracie M.

Kobe P.

Cameron E.

Sarah S.

Louis P.

Luke P.

Harry T.

Estela O.

Amjad H.

Iskandar N.

Bakry N.

Danyaal M.

Ramon R.

Belinda F.

Chanel F.

Amir K.

Printed in Great Britain
by Amazon

28426573R00139